The
MAKE & DO
BIBLE

The
MAKE & DO
BIBLE

Imaginative craft ideas
that bring the stories of the Bible to life

GILLIAN CHAPMAN

CONCORDIA PUBLISHING HOUSE • SAINT LOUIS

CONTENTS

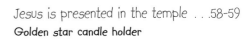

CONTENTS

HOW TO USE THIS BOOK

You will find within this book a wealth of ideas and inspiration that you'll love to use with children at home or in the classroom.

These creative ideas are great for celebrating Christmas and Easter, as well as fun, hands-on ways to bring Old and New Testament stories to life.

Craft ideas vary from simple to more challenging, and each one is designed to be made with inexpensive supplies, using recycled materials where possible. Children will experience the thrill of making something wonderful "out of almost nothing."

To help keep preparation time to a minimum, each project includes:

✷ a lively retelling of the Bible story, suitable for reading aloud to a group

✷ a list of materials needed

✷ clear, step-by-step instructions

✷ a photograph of how the finished article may look.

Ideal for children in first through sixth grades, these crafts will appeal to all ages and interests. All the craft ideas were designed and tested by Gillian Chapman, a well-known author of craft books. Drawing on her experience running children's workshops on making books, masks, and other crafts, Gillian includes helpful tips and recommendations on the pages that follow. It will be helpful for you to read this section before you begin.

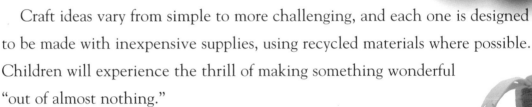

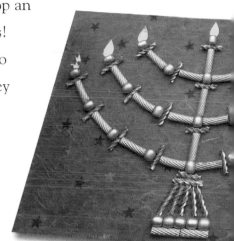

Part of the excitement and satisfaction of *The Make & Do Bible* crafts is when children express their creativity and develop an original slant on an idea or design, whatever the results! Some children (and adults, let's face it) may struggle to follow instructions and lose interest very quickly if they feel an activity is too difficult. Bearing that in mind, the projects in this book can be modified according to an individual's ability. For example, where sewing is involved, you may use craft glue instead; where drawing is involved, you may cut pictures out of magazines.

You will find reproducible patterns and templates in the middle of this book as a helpful starting point. Some of these can be enlarged to produce wall-sized pictures, collages, or displays for homes, classrooms, or churches.

Specific projects, such as harps or helmets, may be used as props for school or worship drama productions. Having read the Bible story and made the crafts, children can enjoy the further dimension of bringing a story to life themselves through drama.

There are endless possibilities for using the ideas in *The Make & Do Bible*. Use them to explore God's Holy Word and discover His salvation promise fulfilled in Jesus. Enjoy them!

BIBLE CRAFT TIPS
Additional practical information

Safety First

Use all tools and equipment with care and respect! Sharp pencils, scissors, and needles can all be dangerous if used incorrectly.

An adult will need to help with carpentry tools and cutting tools.

If you need to use a craft knife, be sure you also use a cutting board.

Shaped scissors

Special scissors with a shaped cutting blade are available for craftwork. You will find them in the scrapbooking section of your local craft store. Use these, or pinking shears, to give paper and fabric a special patterned edge.

Paints

Poster or tempera paints are great for painting on paper and cardstock, and for painting models made from paper pulp and papier mâché. They come in many colors, including metallics. Acrylic paints are better to use on wooden surfaces.

Paints can be mixed on a palette or paper plate. Keep a jar of clean water on hand to clean brushes. Change the water frequently to keep colors looking bright.

For detailed drawings of animals, figures, and faces sketch in the outlines first with pencil, then color in using colored pencils or markers. If you have a set of watercolor paints and a fine brush, use these instead.

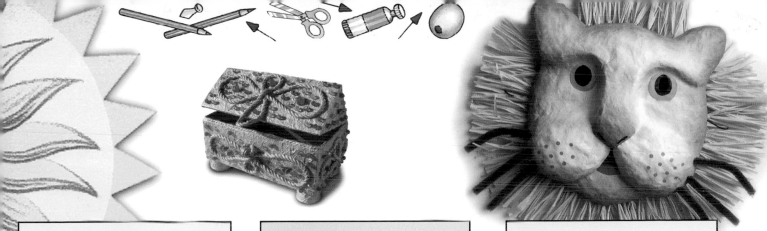

Glues

Craft glue is perfect for most craft projects. It can be diluted for papier mâché projects. It will work on paper, cardstock, and most fabrics — but in most cases it must be used very sparingly. Craft glue is water soluable.

Glue sticks are better for neat finishes but work only on paper and thin cardstock.

When using craft glue to do fine work, such as gluing beads and sequins onto fabric, try to buy the glue in a bottle with a fine tip. If you don't have such a container, pour some of the glue into a small plastic container (like a lid) and use a toothpick to put tiny blobs of glue where it's needed.

Brushes

Keep separate brushes for painting and gluing. Always clean them in warm soapy water after use and let them air dry before putting them away.

Keeping Clean

Make sure all work surfaces are protected with newspaper and all clothing is covered with a paint smock, an old shirt, or an apron. Keep paper towels or an old towel handy for easy clean-ups.

GOD MADE THE WORLD

At the beginning of time, God created a world and filled it with beautiful things.

In the beginning, God made the light and the darkness.

God made big, tall mountains and deep blue seas.

God made plants and flowers and trees and filled the land with them.

God made the round, spinning earth, the red-hot sun, and the silvery moon. He made twinkling stars and planets.

God filled the sea with slippery, shiny fish and the air with birds that sing.

God filled the land with animals of every kind, tall and short, prickly and furry, striped and spotted and patterned.

"Now I will make people," said God. God made a man and a woman in His own image. He made a beautiful garden for them to live in called the Garden of Eden.

God said everything He had made was very good. The God who gave life to all creation will also give us eternal life with Him in Jesus.

Make this wall frieze to illustrate the creation story.

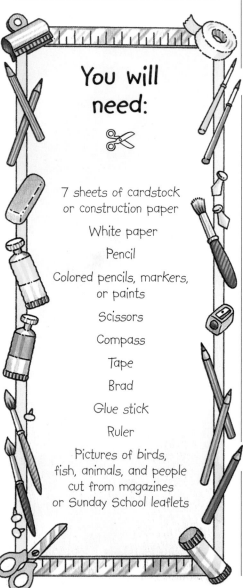

You will need:

✂

7 sheets of cardstock or construction paper

White paper

Pencil

Colored pencils, markers, or paints

Scissors

Compass

Tape

Brad

Glue stick

Ruler

Pictures of birds, fish, animals, and people cut from magazines or Sunday School leaflets

1 Draw a curve across the top of a piece of cardstock or construction paper and cut out. Use this as a template to draw the curve onto the remaining panels. When the panels are cut out, all the panels will be the same shape.

2 Place two panels side by side, leaving a small space between them. Tape the panels together. Join all the panels together in the same way, taping along the front and back of each to make a strong hinge.

3 Draw pictures on white paper to illustrate the first, second, and third days of creation. Color in with paints, markers, or colored pencils. Cut around the drawings so they fit neatly onto the frieze panels and glue in place.

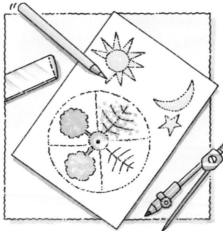

4 Make a seasons wheel for the fourth day of creation. Use the compass to draw a circle on white paper and divide it into four quarters. In each quarter draw a tree at different seasons of the year. Decorate the rest of the page and glue to the frieze

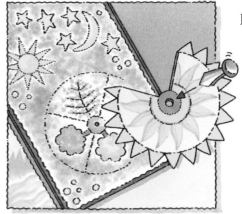

13

5 Draw another circle on white paper and divide into four quarters. Draw a zig-zag pattern around the circle to make a sun shape. Color and cut out, leaving a quarter of the sun cut out. Attach the sun to the center of the tree circle with a brad.

6 Draw pictures to illustrate the fifth, sixth, and seventh days of creation. You can cut out animal pictures from magazines and glue them to your drawings. Carefully cut around the finished drawings and glue them to the correct frieze panels.

Create your own frieze in whatever size and design you like.

Genesis 6:1–9:17

NOAH'S ARK

Noah trusted God to keep him safe in the flood.

Noah was a righteous man, but all around him there was wickedness.

The wonderful world God made was full of sin.

God told Noah He was going to send a great flood.

God told Noah to build a boat and to fill it with two of every kind of animal.

God would keep them safe in the boat when the flood came.

In faith, Noah obeyed God and built a huge wooden boat called an ark. It would float on the waters until the flood was over.

In faith, Noah packed food for his family and all the animals. They were ready for the day when the rain began and the rivers burst into flood.

God kept His promise. Noah and his family were safe. And God will keep all His promises to us too.

You will need:

✂

Sheet of thin colored cardstock

Construction paper

Scissors

Pencil

Glue stick

Scraps of colored paper for decoration

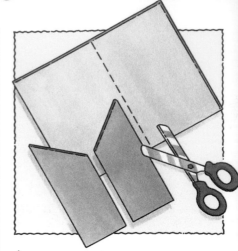

I To make the folder, fold the sheet of cardstock in half, press firmly along the crease and open up. Take a sheet of construction paper, fold in half lengthways, open up, and cut along the fold. Cut the top corners off these two strips.

Make an ark and animal cards to help remember the story of Noah.

2 Use the glue stick to spread a strip of glue along the long side and bottom of the two pieces of construction paper and stick them to the inside of the folder, as shown

3 Cut out construction paper shapes to decorate the front of the folder. Cut out the large roof and hull shapes first and glue them in place using the glue stick. Then add any other details you wish. Don't forget to decorate the inside of the folder too.

4 To make the cards, cut a sheet of construction paper in half, then fold each piece in half. Decorate the cards with simple animal shapes cut from colored paper. Start by drawing and cutting out body shapes, then heads. Place the pieces on the card first before gluing to make sure they are the right size. Be sure the fold is at the top.

5 Make the animals as colorful as possible. Cut out features like ears, tails, tusks, spots, and stripes, and use the gluestick to glue them neatly into place. When all the pieces are stuck down, shape the top corners of the card and cut out the space between the legs, cutting through both sides of the card.

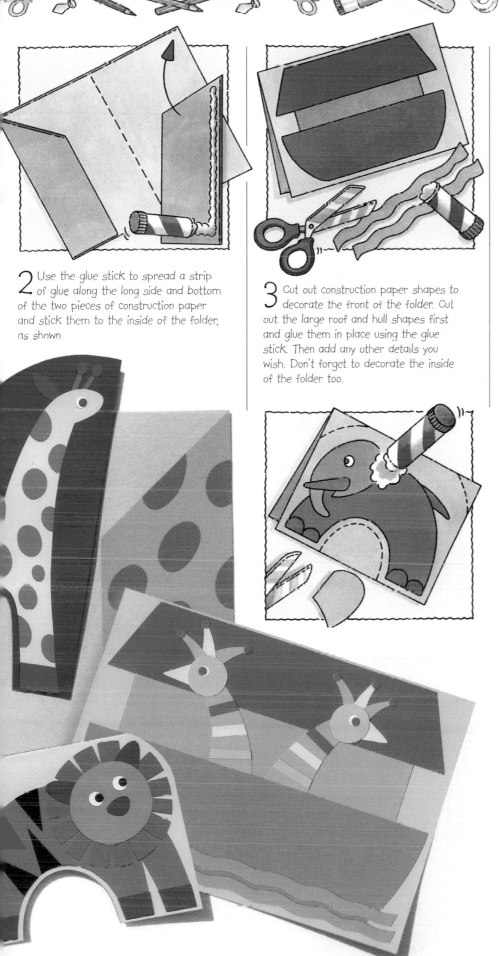

6 The tall giraffe card is made in the same way, but the fold of the card runs along the left side. Small gift tags are made from a single thickness of cardstock, threaded with string. Keep all your animal cards in the ark folder so they are handy for last-minute gifts!

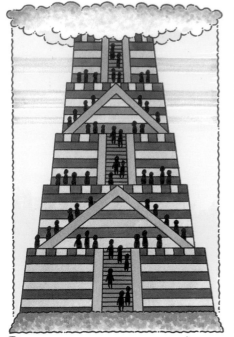

THE TOWER OF BABEL

Genesis 11:1–9

You will need:

Cardboard tubes of different sizes with plastic lids (e.g. empty potato chip or cookie tubes)

Glue stick

Scraps of colored paper

Tape

Sheet of wrapping paper

Scissors

Colored felt-tipped pens

Colored stickers or stamps for added decoration

Words, messages, and phrases in as many languages as you can find

The people said, "Let's build a tower that reaches to the sky."

At first, all the people in the world spoke the same language. They moved about from place to place, looking for somewhere to settle.

"Let's make our own city with bricks," they said. So they baked bricks in the hot sun.

When they had enough bricks, they took some tar to stick them together. They started to build their city.

"Let's build a tower that reaches to the sky!" they said. "Then everyone will know how clever and important we are."

But God saw what they were planning. He knew they were forgetting about Him and the way He wanted them to live. So the God of grace mixed up their language. They couldn't understand each other any more! It all sounded like babble. God scattered the self-centered people all over the earth. God preserved those who loved Him and the generations of families from which the Messiah would be born.

When you are copying words or characters in a language that is unfamiliar to you, be very careful, as a small slip of the pen may give the word the wrong meaning or make it completely meaningless!

Make these tower boxes and decorate them with foreign stamps or writing.

TOWER PENCIL CASE

1 Before you begin, make sure the cardboard tube is clean inside and tall enough to hold all your pencils! Cover the tube with wrapping paper. Lay the tube on the paper to measure the correct width and trim the paper to size.

2 Spread a thin layer of glue on the paper using the glue stick and carefully wrap the paper around the tube. Secure the end of the paper with tape.

3 Write out words and phrases in different languages on small scraps of colored paper. Either copy these from books or, if you have friends who speak a different language, ask them to write out messages for you to copy.

TOWER DESK TIDY

4 Glue the paper messages to the tube along with small paper shapes, colored stickers, or stamps to decorate the tubes. Don't forget to decorate the lid.

5 This is made in the same way as the pencil case, but you don't need such a tall tube or a lid. Choose a container that will hold all your writing equipment so you can see exactly where they are when you need them!

GOD'S PROMISE TO ABRAHAM

God told Abram to count the stars in the sky.

Abram trusted and followed God. He left his home to settle in a new land which God had showed him.

God promised to make Abram's family very important. The problem was, Abram and his wife Sarai could not have children. Without children, their family could not grow any bigger.

One day God told Abram that he would have a son and a very large family. "Look at the stars and try to count them," said God. "You will have as many people in your family as the number of stars you can see."

Years went by. Abram was now an old man, but in faith he trusted God and believed His special promise.

When Abram was ninety-nine years

old, God's promise started to come true!

God gave Abram a new son and a new name — Abraham.

Many years later, Jesus, a descendant of Abraham, was born. He came to make many people God's children through His life, death, and resurrection.

You will need:

✂

Thin cardstock

Compass

Ruler and pencil

Scissors

Pieces of felt

Embroidery floss and needle

Craft glue

Felt-tipped pen

Assorted beads and sequins

Acrylic or cotton stuffing

Make this star mobile to help you remember God's promise to Abraham.

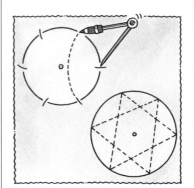

1 First, you will need to make some star templates. Use the compass to draw a 6-inch diameter circle on the cardstock. Keeping the position of the compass points the same, mark six points around the circumference of the circle. Draw lines from point to point with a ruler.

2 Make two more star shapes from 4-inch and 2-inch circles and cut them out. Use these templates to make stars from felt. Place the template on the felt, draw around it with a felt tipped pen and cut it out with scissors. You will need two 6-inch stars, six 4-inch stars, and six 2-inch stars.

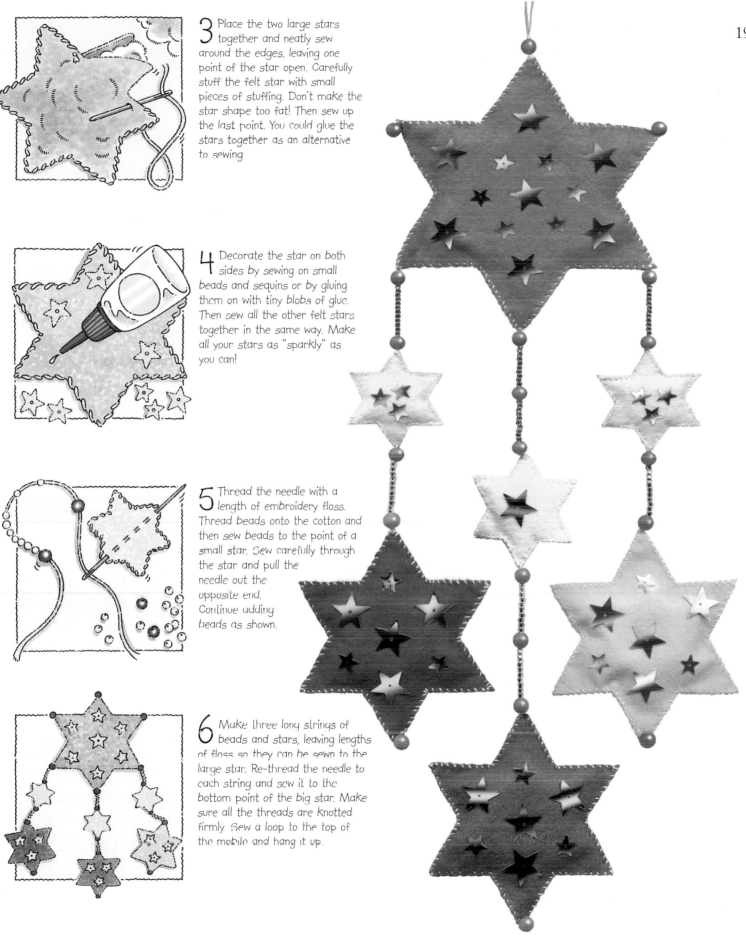

3 Place the two large stars together and neatly sew around the edges, leaving one point of the star open. Carefully stuff the felt star with small pieces of stuffing. Don't make the star shape too fat! Then sew up the last point. You could glue the stars together as an alternative to sewing

4 Decorate the star on both sides by sewing on small beads and sequins or by gluing them on with tiny blobs of glue. Then sew all the other felt stars together in the same way. Make all your stars as "sparkly" as you can!

5 Thread the needle with a length of embroidery floss. Thread beads onto the cotton and then sew beads to the point of a small star. Sew carefully through the star and pull the needle out the opposite end. Continue adding beads as shown.

6 Make three long strings of beads and stars, leaving lengths of floss so they can be sewn to the large star. Re-thread the needle to each string and sew it to the bottom point of the big star. Make sure all the threads are knotted firmly. Sew a loop to the top of the mobile and hang it up.

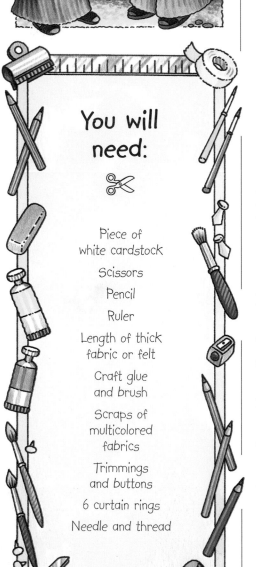

You will need:

✂

Piece of
white cardstock

Scissors

Pencil

Ruler

Length of thick
fabric or felt

Craft glue
and brush

Scraps of
multicolored
fabrics

Trimmings
and buttons

6 curtain rings

Needle and thread

Genesis 24:10–67

REBEKAH'S SURPRISE

Make this colorful banner and think of Rebekah watering all those camels!

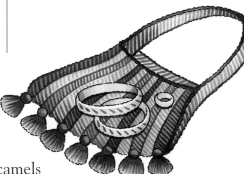

Every evening Rebekah fetched water from the well.

One day, she saw a man standing at the well with his camels.

"Please give me a drink," he said.

Rebekah offered him some water and then gave the thirsty camels a drink too. They had travelled a long way.

Then Rebekah had a surprise! The man took a beautiful gold ring and gold bracelets out of his bag and put them on her.

"Please take me to your father's house," he said. So they set off to see Rebekah's family.

There was another surprise. The man said he was a servant of Abraham and he had come to find a wife for his master's son, Isaac. He had prayed and asked God to help him. Now he asked if Rebekah would go with him and become Isaac's wife. Rebekah agreed.

Rebekah and several of her helpers traveled back to Canaan. God helped Rebekah and the servants to make the right choice.

God had made a new family.

1 Draw a simple outline of a camel on the white card and cut it out carefully. Use this shape as a pattern to make all the fabric camels.

3 Make the banner from a strip of fabric long enough for a row of ten camels. To make a rough calculation of the length, measure the width of one camel and multiply it by ten.

5 When all the camels are glued in place, decorate the banner with small buttons, beads, or trimmings. Glue other trim to the top and bottom edges.

2 Lay the pattern on a piece of fabric, draw around the shape, and cut out the camel. Repeat this until you have ten camels cut from different fabrics.

4 Glue the camels to the background with small blobs of glue. Start at the left side of the banner and overlap the camels so the tail overlaps the neck of the previous one.

6 Sew the curtain rings at intervals along the top edge of the banner. These represent the jewelry given to Rebekah at the well and can be used to hang the banner.

22

JACOB AND ESAU
Esau trades his blessing.

Esau and Jacob were twin brothers. Esau was born first, which meant that when their father died, Esau would be given all that their father owned and a special blessing. Jacob wanted this blessing to be his.

One day, when Esau came home from hunting, he was very hungry. He could smell a delicious stew that Jacob had been cooking.

"Give me some of that stew," he asked Jacob.

"Only if you promise to let me be the one who gets Dad's special blessing," said Jacob.

Esau didn't care about his special blessing, so he promised to let Jacob have their father's blessing. Esau only cared about his hungry tummy!

Jacob and Esau both sinned. Sin caused sadness and eventually separated the two brothers. We sin too and sin separates us from others and from God. But we have Jesus, our blessed Savior, who forgives our sins and brings us close with God again.

1 Sketch out your design on paper. Draw the stewpot and the ladle. Decorate the pot with designs and have some steam rising out of the top. Finally, draw a patterned border around your design.

You will need:

✄

Sketching paper and pencil

Felt-tipped pen

Sheet of sandpaper and thick cardstock

Scissors

Craft glue

Glue spreader or brush

Collage materials: dried beans, lentils, green split peas, pasta shapes and sunflower seeds*.

* Please remind children that raw beans are not edible and small peas could be a choking hazard.

2 Glue the sandpaper to the card-stock and let dry. The sandpaper will give the collage a lovely textured background. Trim the sandpaper to the same size as your picture.

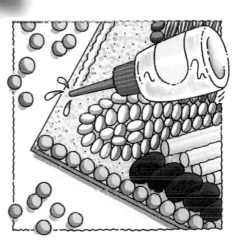

Make this collage stewpot and think about Jacob & Esau.

5 Spread glue over the center of the stewpot and fill in the shape with rows of different colored beans and pasta shapes.

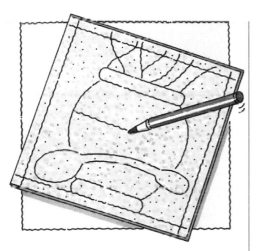

3 Following the design, sketch the outlines of the main shapes onto the sandpaper using a felt tipped pen. This will give you guidelines when you start assembling the collage.

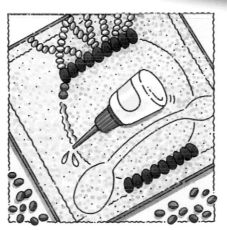

4 Begin with the main shapes. Spread glue along the outlines and press the beans into the glue. Work around the stewpot and the lines of steam and fill in the ladle.

6 Spread the glue along the lines of the border pattern and press a row of beans around the edge. The glue will dry clear so there shouldn't be any blobs of glue showing when it dries.

JOSEPH'S COAT

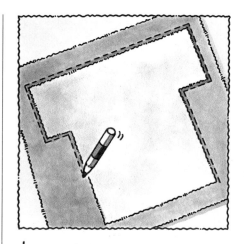

You will need:

✂

Large piece of scrap fabric for patchwork lining

Felt-tipped pen

Smaller scraps of multicolored fabrics

Scissors

Sewing needle, thread, and pins

Craft glue and brush

Tapestry needle and colored yarns

Extra trimmings, buttons, and beads for decoration

Favorite Bible verses written on pieces of paper

Length of dowel

2 wood balls or large beads

Joseph was given a wonderful coat by his father.

Jacob was an old man who had twelve sons. He loved them all, but he had a special love for Joseph, who was born to Jacob in his old age.

As a special present, Jacob gave Joseph a wonderful coat to wear. The coat made the brothers jealous. But Joseph forgave his brothers for their anger.

God has a special love for His children too. He sent His only Son, Jesus, to die on the cross for the sins of all. Those who believe in Jesus as their Savior have an even more wonderful coat — the robe of Christ's righteousness.

Use a felt-tipped pen to draw a large "T" shape onto the fabric and cut it out. Then use the shape as a pattern to cut out a second identical shape. These shapes will form the lining of the patch-work hanging, so their size and shape will determine the size of the finished project.

Make this patchwork hanging to help you remember the special coat Joseph wore.

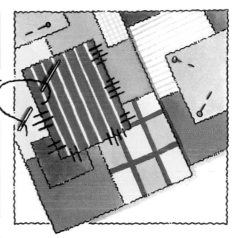

5 When the patchwork is dry, pin some larger patches to the coat to make pockets. Sew these in place with colored yarn These pockets will hold the Bible verses you've written.

6 Finishing Touches: use trimmings and buttons to make the patchwork coat as colorful as possible. To make a hanger, thread the dowel through the sleeves so about an inch shows from each sleeve. Have an adult cut the dowel to size. Glue a ball or bead onto each end. Tie colored yarns to the dowel to hang up the coat. See page 87 for tassel making instructions.

3 Cut lots of square patches from your collection of fabric scraps. They can be all different sizes. Glue the patches to the lining, starting at the bottom. Use the glue very sparingly!

2 Lay the two shapes on top of each other and pin together. Cut the top layer in half along the center and cut around the collar. Sew the shapes together across the shoulders and along the sides as shown, or glue them together.

4 Work up both sides of the coat, keeping the two halves separate. Overlap the patches so the lining fabric is completely covered. If you have enough patches, also cover the back of the coat.

Genesis 37:1–11

Joseph's dreams made his brothers jealous.

JOSEPH'S DREAMS

Joseph's brothers were jealous of Joseph. He was their father's favorite and had been given a wonderful coat.

To make things worse, Joseph started telling them stories about odd dreams he had been having.

"We were all in the field tying the wheat into sheaves," said Joseph. "Suddenly my sheaf got up and yours stood round it in a circle. Your sheaves bowed down to mine!"

The brothers didn't like the sound of that at all! Or what came next…

"I've had another dream!" said Joseph.

"I dreamed I saw the sun, moon, and eleven stars all bowing down to me!"

Joseph's brothers didn't want Joseph to be more important than they were. They started to plan how to get rid of him.

During all this time God was planning to use Joseph in a way that would help many people.

Even when we don't understand our life, God has plans for our good too. God loves and cares for us.

You will need:

✂

A small notebook with a plain cover

Scissors

Wrapping paper and textured papers

Glue stick

Dried grasses

Craft glue and brush

Sheets of thin cardstock to make cards and bookmarks (optional)

1 Place the open notebook on top of the wrapping paper with the wrong side of the paper facing up. Hold the notebook in place by placing a heavier book on top of it. Trim any excess paper to approximately 1" (or a ruler's width) all round.

2 Close the notebook, keeping it in place on the paper. Spread glue over the front cover using the glue stick. Then open the book so the paper sticks to the cover.

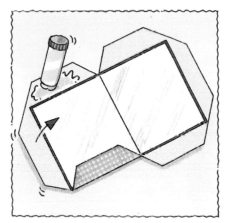

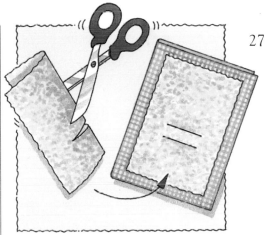

3 Close the notebook again from the back and cover the back and the spine with glue. Open the notebook so the paper sticks to the back cover and spine.

4 Trim excess paper from the corners and spine as shown here. Crease the paper flaps and glue them to the inside of the covers. Smooth the new cover with your hands, making sure it sticks firmly.

5 Take a piece of textured paper slightly smaller than the notebook cover and cut two small slits across the center as shown. Glue around the edge of the paper and stick it to the front cover, leaving the slits unglued.

Decorate a notebook with wheat or dried grasses to remind you of Joseph's dreams.

6 Weave dried grasses or wheat through the slits and glue them in place with small blobs of glue. Look at the ideas pictured here and use the same method to decorate greetings cards and bookmarks.

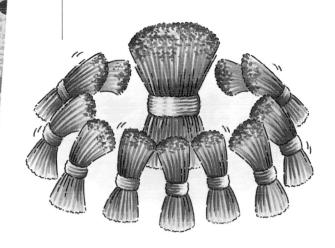

28

JOSEPH INTERPRETS DREAMS

Genesis 40:1–23

God gave Joseph a message for the baker and wine steward.

When Joseph was in prison in Egypt, he met the king's chief baker and the king's wine steward. They were prisoners too.

They had unusual dreams. Joseph said he would listen and see if God would help him understand what the dreams meant. The wine steward spoke first:

"I dreamt there was a grapevine with three branches. I squeezed the grapes into the king's cup and gave it to him to drink."

Joseph said, "In three days the king will let you out of prison and give you back your old job. Please remember me when you are out of prison and tell the king about me."

Next it was the baker's turn: "I was carrying three bread baskets on my head. In the top basket were all sorts of pastries for the king, and the birds were eating them all up."

Joseph told him: "In three days the king will let you out of

You will need:

✂

Large mixing bowl

Mixing spoon

11oz. plain flour

11oz. salt

7fl oz. water

1 tablespoon oil

Poster paints

Paint brush

Sifter

Baking tray covered with wax paper or baker's parchment

Wire cooling rack

Rolling pin, plastic knife to cut and shape the dough

*Adult help to use the oven and bake the dough

1 Sift the flour and salt into the bowl. Pour in the water, adding a little at a time while stirring the mixture with the spoon. Then add the oil.

2 Knead the mixture with your fingers until it is smooth. If the dough is too wet, add more flour and if it is too dry, add a little more water.

prison, but he will cut off your head."

The poor baker was very worried. But it all happened just as Joseph had said.

Later the wine steward would remember Joseph. God would use Joseph to help the king interpret his dreams and later to help an entire nation.

Make this grapevine out of salt dough and paint it to remind you of the wine steward's dream.

3 Make three long sausage shapes from the dough by rolling it on a flat surface. Place the shapes on the baking tray covered with the wax paper or parchment. Twist or braid them together at one end to form the trunk of the vine with three branches.

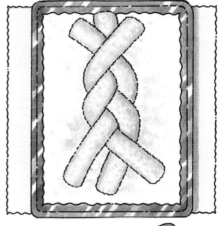

4 Roll out a piece of dough using the rolling pin and use the plastic knife to cut out some leaf shapes. Place these on the branches. Then make lots of small balls of dough with your fingers and stick these together on the branches to make the bunches of grapes. Brushing water on the dough will help the pieces stick together.

5 When you have finished making the grapevine, ask an adult to bake it for you. Preheat the oven to 250° and bake the dough until hard. This may take up to 5 hours.

6 Carefully slide the grapevine from the baking tray onto the wire rack to cool. When it is completely cool, paint it with the poster paints.

Exodus 2:1–10

MOSES IN THE BULRUSHES

Baby Moses was hidden in a basket on the river to keep him safe.

1 Paint the cardstock on both sides with a colorful abstract design. Make sure the first side is completely dry before painting the reverse!

Weave this simple basket and imagine baby Moses being hidden inside.

You will need:

✂

Large sheet of thin white cardstock

Paints and paint brush

Ruler, pencil, and scissors

Blunt needle and colored twine

Tape

2 Measure and mark the card into 1 inch wide strips and carefully cut them out. You will need 8 strips 12 inches long and 4 strips 16 inches long to begin weaving the basket. (A paper cutter works great for this.)

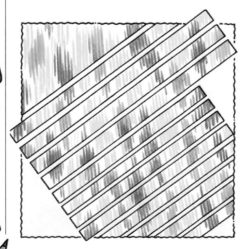

3 Lay the long strips side by side, as shown, and weave the shorter strips in and out to form the base of the basket. Keep all the strips neatly in place. Weight down the long ends with a book to help keep them aligned.

In Egypt there was a cruel king. He had many slaves and he treated them badly. There were so many slaves that the king began to fear that they would turn against him.

So he ordered all the baby boys to be thrown into the river and drowned.

But one woman had a plan to love and save her son. She hid her baby until he was three months old. Then she made a special basket out of reeds. She placed her baby in God's care, putting him into the basket and setting it

among the bulrushes at the side of the river.

The baby's sister, Miriam, watched close by.

Later the king's daughter came to the river to bathe. She saw the basket, heard a tiny voice, and found the baby. The princess wanted to save him.

Miriam stepped out from the bulrushes.

"I know who can nurse the baby," said Miriam. And she fetched her own mother.

The baby was called Moses and was looked after by his mother until he was old enough to live in the royal palace.

God has saved us through Jesus. He rescues us from the dangers of sin, death, and the devil. He keeps us forever as His own dear children.

4 Bend up each strip so it forms a right angle to the base. Do this along each side of the basket.

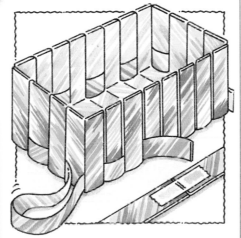

5 Measure and cut 3 long strips, 1 inch wide and 28 inches long to weave the sides of the basket. If the strips are not long enough, join two together with tape.

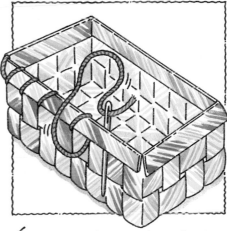

6 Measure and cut a final strip that is 2 inches wide and 28 inches long. Fold it in half lengthways and fold it over the top edge of the basket. Sew it in place with the colored twine as shown above.

God told Moses to make a special lampstand.

THE GOLDEN LAMPSTAND

God had helped Moses set His people free from slavery in Egypt.

Now God wanted Moses to make special things to go inside the tabernacle, or tent of meeting, where God would meet with His people. These were the Covenant Box (which contained the two stone tablets with God's commandments written on them), a table, and a lampstand.

The lampstand, or menora, was made of pure gold, with seven branches. The people brought the best olive oil for the precious lampstand. It would burn from evening until morning. The light from the lamp represented the glory of the Lord as reflected in the lives of His children.

Through God's Spirit, His children today also reflect the love of God—especially the love He showed in sending His Son to be our Savior from sin.

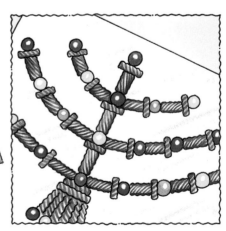

You will need:

Sketching paper and pencil

Wooden beads

Gold poster paint and brush

Dried pasta shapes

Thin knitting needles or kabob sticks

20" x 14" thick cardboard

22" x 16" dark blue fabric or paper

Craft glue and brush

Scraps of gold paper

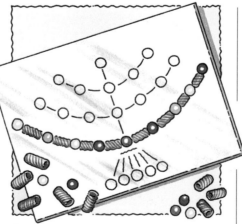

1 First sketch a simple outline of the lampstand on the paper or fabric. Then start to place the pasta shapes and beads over the pencil design.

2 When you have finished arranging the pasta and beads, you will know exactly how many pieces you need to paint. Take off all the pieces for painting.

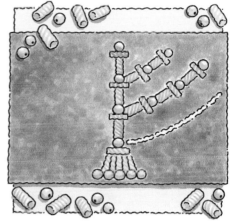

5 Follow your sketch and begin to arrange the golden pasta shapes and beads onto the backing card. First glue the central stem of the lampstand in place in the middle of the card.

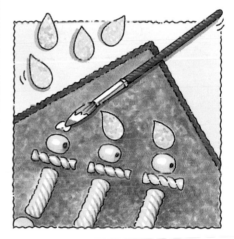

6 Glue all the shapes in place and let the lampstand picture dry. Cut small flame shapes from gold paper and glue them above each branch of the lampstand to represent a burning flame.

Make this golden lampstand picture and imagine the one in God's tent of meeting.

3 If you thread the beads onto thin knitting needles or kabob sticks, it will make them easier to paint. Pasta absorbs the paint very quickly so it will not take long for them to dry.

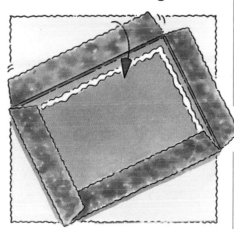

4 Take the cardboard and spread the surface with glue. Glue the fabric or paper to the surface, carefully smoothing it flat. Turn the cardboard over and neatly fold and glue the edges of the fabric to the back.

34

GIDEON'S VICTORY
'A sword for the Lord and for Gideon!'

God chose Gideon to be a mighty warrior in Israel. He knew that God was on his side and would help him defeat the Midianite army. God gave Gideon a plan. Each soldier had a trumpet and a jar with a burning torch inside.

"This is what we must do," he told his army. "When I get to the edge of the camp, watch me and copy what I do. When I blow my trumpet, blow yours too and shout, 'A sword for the Lord and for Gideon!'"

So Gideon and his men came to the edge of the camp in the middle of the night. Gideon blew his trumpet and broke his jar.

Then everyone broke their jars, picked up their trumpets, and shouted: "A sword for the Lord and for Gideon!"

The enemy army ran away! Gideon won a great victory for the Lord.

God chose Gideon to do a great work, and God helped Gideon do it. In the same way, God has chosen us to be His helpers and He keeps His promises to help us.

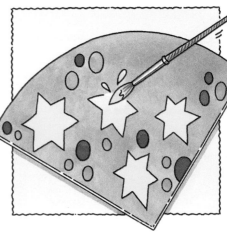

You will need:

✂

Sheets of thin colored cardstock and paper

Pencil

Tape

Scissors

Length of thick cord

Craft glue and brush

Black felt-tipped pen

Colored string or yarn

Paints and brush, stickers, stars or shapes to decorate the trumpet

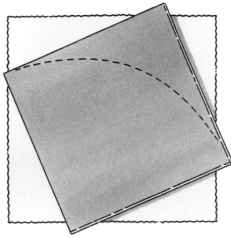

1 Take a square of colored cardstock and draw an arc connecting opposite corners, as shown. Cut away the excess using the scissors.

2 Paint the trumpet while the card is flat. You can also decorate it with colored shapes and stars or stickers.

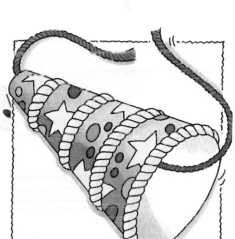

5 When you get to the wide end of the trumpet, glue the cord around the edge of the opening and allow it to dry. When it is dry, thread a length of string through the trumpet and tie the ends together. You can hang up the finished trumpet using this string!

Make this trumpet to remember God's plan for Gideon's victory.

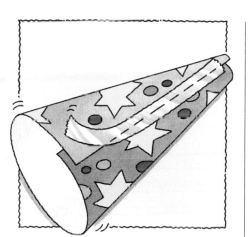

3 Roll the card into a trumpet shape and join the edges together firmly with tape.

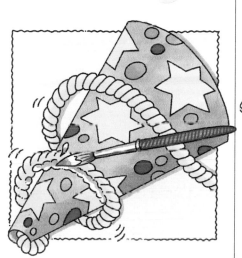

4 Tuck one end of the cord into the hole at the small end of the trumpet and glue in place. Then carefully wrap the cord around the trumpet, gluing it in place as you go with small blobs of glue.

6 Cut out some long curly shapes from the colored paper and draw musical notes along the length with the black felt-tipped pen. Stick them just inside the trumpet with tape so they curl out of the opening.

THE STRENGTH OF SAMSON

Judges 14:5–6; 16:4–30

Nobody knew why Samson was so strong!

Samson was very strong. He once fought a lion and killed it with his own hands! God had made him strong. But nobody knew the secret of his great strength.

One day Samson met a woman called Delilah. Samson's enemies paid her to find out the secret of his strength. Delilah kept asking him until finally he could stand it no longer.

"If I cut off my hair, I will be made weak," said Samson.

So when Samson was asleep, Delilah called to his enemies and they cut off his hair. At once his strength left him. He was blinded and thrown into prison in chains. In prison Samson's hair began to grow again.

Samson's enemies had a big party because they had captured Samson. Samson prayed to God to give him his strength back. God did just that and Samson pushed over the pillars of the building.

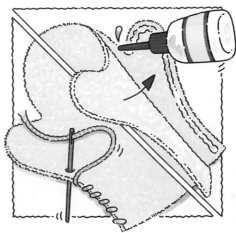

The roof fell. God had heard Samson's prayer and used him in a mighty way. Samson died, but he took many of God's enemies with him. Jesus is like Samson only greater. By giving His life, He defeated sin, death, and the devil for us.

You will need:

✂

Two 10" squares of yellow felt

Black felt-tipped pen

Sewing needle and thread

Scraps of orange, red, light and dark brown, blue and white felt

Scissors

Sketching paper, pencil, and tracing paper

Scraps of yarn for whiskers

Craft glue in a small plastic bottle with a tip and a toothpick

Scrap cardstock

1 Place your hand on a piece of yellow felt and use it as a guide to make the puppet shape. Draw around your hand with the felt-tipped pen and make the shape ¾"–1" bigger than the hand. Make sure that your thumb and little finger fit into the two arms of the puppet shape and cut it

2 Make a second identical felt glove shape and join the two shapes together, leaving the bottom open. Either sew the two pieces together or glue them using the tip to spread a thin line of glue around the edge of one of the gloves.

3 Sketch your own lion face design and trace over it. Use the tracing to mark the shapes on felt and cut them all out.

4 Start by cutting out the mane from brown felt, the face shape from yellow felt, and two orange ear shapes. Glue the two ears to the mane, then glue the mane to the top part of the glove. Glue the yellow face to the center of the mane. Place a piece of cardstock inside the glove to prevent glue from soaking through to the bottom layer.

5 Carefully cut out the other smaller felt shapes—a brown mouth, 2 white teeth and large eye circles, 2 small blue eyes, 2 fierce brown eyebrows, 2 orange muzzle shapes, a red tongue, and a brown nose. Use a toothpick to dab small blobs of glue onto the shapes and stick them to the face. Begin with the eyes, then the mouth and teeth. Glue the lengths of yarn across the face and glue the muzzle and nose over the top.

6 Finally, cut out a long tail shape from the orange felt. Glue one end to the back of the puppet and the other end to the front. Cut out a shaggy brown felt shape and glue it over the front end of the tail. Cut out two orange paws and glue them to the ends of both arms.

Make this lion glove puppet to remind you of Samson's great strength.

1 Samuel 16:14–23

DAVID'S HARP
David helped the king by playing his harp.

King Saul was a very troubled man. He used to be happy, but he had not done what God had told him to do. Now he felt terrible.

His servants thought it would help him to listen to some music.

"There is a boy in Bethlehem," said one servant, "who is very good at playing the harp. His name is David."

They told Saul and he asked them to fetch David.

David set off from home to see the king and play his harp.

King Saul listened to him playing the harp and suddenly felt much better.

"Stay here," he said to David. "I wish to hear more."

So David served King Saul. Whenever the king felt terrible, David would play beautiful music on his harp.

David used the gifts God had given him for others. He also used them later when he became a godly king.

We can also use our gifts and talents to serve God and others, now and in the future.

You will need:

✂️

Adult help to cut the wood and to supervise the construction of the harp.

Sandpaper to smooth any rough edges.

Pieces of wood:
9" × 7" × ¼"
20" × 1" × ¼"
17½" × 1" × ¼"
15½" × 1" × ¼"

8 brass eyelets

Nylon fishing line or nylon guitar strings

Tools:
Saw, hammer, and small nails

Paints, palette, and brush

Pencil and ruler

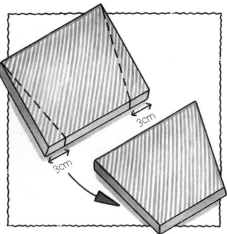

1 Take the rectangle of wood, measure and mark the dimensions as shown, then ask an adult to saw the wood to size. This is the base of the harp.

2 Take the two longer lengths of wood and position them on the base as shown, lining up the two ends. Carefully nail into place.

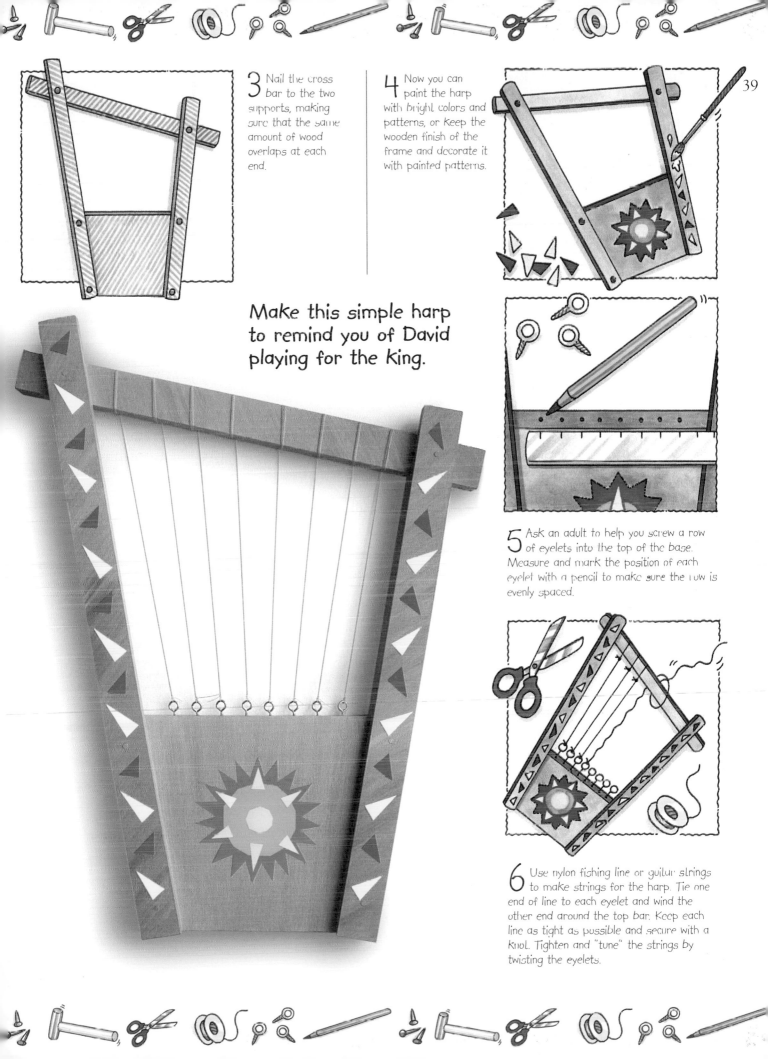

3 Nail the cross bar to the two supports, making sure that the same amount of wood overlaps at each end.

4 Now you can paint the harp with bright colors and patterns, or keep the wooden finish of the frame and decorate it with painted patterns.

Make this simple harp to remind you of David playing for the King.

5 Ask an adult to help you screw a row of eyelets into the top of the base. Measure and mark the position of each eyelet with a pencil to make sure the row is evenly spaced.

6 Use nylon fishing line or guitar strings to make strings for the harp. Tie one end of line to each eyelet and wind the other end around the top bar. Keep each line as tight as possible and secure with a knot. Tighten and "tune" the strings by twisting the eyelets.

DAVID AND GOLIATH

God helped David, a shepherd boy, kill the Philistine enemy!

Who could fight a giant?

Goliath, the champion of the Philistine army, asked King Saul to find a man who would fight him. But Goliath was over 9 feet tall! Nobody in Saul's army even dared to try!

For forty days, Goliath asked the army, "Who will fight me?"

Then one day, David left his sheep to take some food to his brothers, who were soldiers in the camp.

David heard Goliath shouting. He couldn't understand why no one stepped forward. David had often fought wild animals to protect his sheep.

"God will help me fight Goliath," said David, "as He has helped me protect my sheep."

"Then put on my armor and take my sword," King Saul said. But they were much too heavy for David.

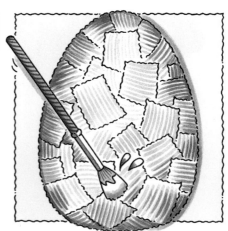

God gave David a special plan. David went to the river and chose five smooth stones. He took out his sling, then set off to face Goliath. David relied on God's strength as he came to fight in the name of the Lord Almighty. He whirled the sling round his head and threw one of the stones at Goliath. It hit him on the forehead and killed the giant!

The Philistines ran away, chased by King Saul's army. God was with David and gave the Israelites a victory! God also blesses us, calls us to rely on Him, and uses us to do His will.

You will need:

✂

A large rounded stone

Newspaper

Craft glue and brush

Bowl to mix the papier-mâché

Corrugated cardboard

Scissors

Bronze and colored poster paints and brush

Scraps of felt, string, and paper for decoration

A small stick

1 Wrap the stone with strips of glued newspaper. Build up the newspaper strips until you have a body shape that is flatter at the base with a rounded top. Allow to dry.

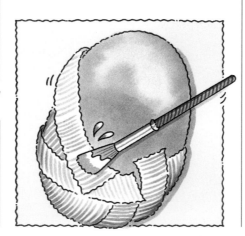

2 Refine the shape by gluing smaller pieces of newspaper to the body. Keep the surface as smooth as possible.

5 Cut two hands from brown felt and glue these to the arms. Cut strips of felt from another color to make cuffs and glue them on to hide the joins. Glue the arms to the body. Then make Goliath's feathered headdress from blue felt.

3 Cut the feet shape from the cardboard. The feet must stick out from under the body. Glue the body to the feet and build up the shapes of the feet with pieces of papier-mâché

4 When the papier mâché is completely dry, the figure can be painted. Make Goliath's face as fierce as possible and give him a large bushy beard. Cut two arms from felt in a color to match Goliath's armor.

Use a stone to make this paperweight and remember how God helped David.

6 Make Goliath's spear from a stick with a paper point, attached with string, as shown here. Cut the dagger from paper. Glue both to Goliath's hands.

DANIEL IN THE LIONS' DEN

Daniel 6

You will need:

✂️

White sketching paper

Ruler

Rolling pin and board

Newspaper

Paints and paint brush

Raffia and large blunt needle

Length of thin elastic

Pencil

Modeling clay and cutting tool/blunt knife

Plastic wrap

Craft glue and brush

Scissors

Chenille wire

Daniel was thrown into a pit of lions, but God kept him safe.

Daniel was taken to live in a country far away from his home. He worked hard and the king made him a leader.

But Daniel's enemies were jealous and plotted against him. They asked the king to make a rule that no one should pray to anyone but the king for thirty days, or they would be thrown into a pit of lions. And the king did. In faith, Daniel still prayed to God. He was arrested and taken to be fed to the lions!

The king was horrified because Daniel was his friend. He hoped

Make this lion mask and pretend to be one of the lions in the pit.

1 First, plan the design for your lion mask. Draw a large circle the same size as your face. Add simple features: eyes, ears, nose, whiskers, and mane.

2 With your drawing as a guide, make a simple clay mold for the papier-mâché mask.

Roll out the clay to a thickness of 1". Cut out a large circle for the face. Then add triangles for the ears, a wedge shape for the nose, and small circles for the cheeks. Roll out sausage shapes for the eyebrows.

3 Use your shapes to build up the lion's features and make a 3D mold. Then cover the clay mold with plastic wrap.

4 Tear up small strips of newspaper. Use a diluted solution of glue to cover the mold with six layers of paper. Make sure each layer covers evenly. Allow to dry completely.

5 Let the mask dry completely. Then carefully pull up the plastic wrap to remove the mask from the mold. Trim around the mask with scissors and cut out the eye holes. Paint the mask.

6 Use a sharp pencil or needle to make holes around the mask. Thread the needle with lengths of raffia and sew them through the holes, knotting each at the back. Use chenille wire for whiskers. Make two holes on each side of the mask, thread elastic through, and adjust to fit your head.

that Daniel would somehow survive.

As soon as morning came, the king went back to the lions' pit and called, "Daniel! Has your God saved you?"

Daniel called back, "Yes! I'm alive!" God had sent an angel to stop the lions from harming him.

The king released Daniel and punished Daniel's enemies.

Daniel was free to pray to the one true God for the rest of his life, and the king honored Daniel's God who had the power to save.

Like Daniel we trust in God's mighty power to save. Christ strengthens us through His Word and sacraments so we can give a bold witness to our faith.

JONAH AND THE BIG FISH

Jonah was swallowed up by a big fish.

You will need:

✂

3 sheets of cardstock

Scissors

Paints or colored pencils

Sharp pencil

5 brads

String

Weight (e.g., key, metal washer, or similar)

Ruler

Tape

1 Draw an underwater scene on the first sheet of cardstock. This is the background for the picture. Use paints or pencils to color waves and fish. Then draw a similar watery scene half-way up the second sheet of card and cut it out. This is the foreground.

2 On the third sheet, draw a big fish with a large open mouth, as shown here, and a small figure of Jonah. Use paints or pencils to color them in, then carefully cut out both shapes.

3 Measure a point in the center of the fish and make a small hole (X) with a sharp pencil. Measure and mark two more holes (A and B) on either side of X.

God told Jonah to go to Nineveh and call His people to repentance. Jonah was afraid and ran away from God.

He went aboard a ship and set sail. But God sent a mighty storm. The sailors thought they would all drown.

Jonah knew he was the cause of their trouble so he told them to throw him into the sea.

The storm stopped as soon as Jonah was overboard.

But God saved Jonah. He sent an enormous fish to swallow up Jonah.

He lived inside the fish for three days and nights.

When the fish spat him out, Jonah went to Nineveh and preached God's grace. When they heard God's word, the people of Nineveh repented.

God, who desires all people to be saved, gives His church the Good News of repentance and forgiveness of sins in Christ.

Make this moving fish picture to remind you of the story of Jonah.

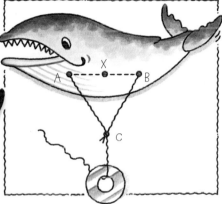

5 Thread a length of string through holes in the fish at A and B, and tie the string at C. Then tie the weight to the end of the string.

6 To assemble the picture, push a brad through the center hole in the foreground, through the hole X in the fish, and through the hole in the background. Secure the brad at the back with tape. Glue Jonah to the background, behind the open mouth. Attach the foreground to the background at the corners with four brads.

Pin the picture firmly to a wall or bulletin board. Swing the weight and watch the fish swallow Jonah!

4 Place the background scene and the foreground on top of each other so the bottom edges are exactly in line, and hold together. Measure the point in the center of the cards, at the top edge of the foreground, and make a hole through both cards with a sharp pencil.

AN ANGEL VISITS MARY

Luke 1:26–38

News of the baby King!

Mary lived in a little town called Nazareth. She was soon to be married to Joseph, a carpenter. But one day she had a visitor with some surprising news that changed Mary's life forever!

God sent the angel Gabriel to talk to Mary. "Greetings!" said the angel. "Don't be afraid. God has chosen you to have a baby, and He will be God's Son. You shall name Him Jesus. He will be the King forever."

"I am God's servant," said Mary. "I will do as God asks."

The angel left, and Mary sang a song of praise to God because soon she would have a baby and that baby would be God in human form, the Savior.

Make this pop-up card as a reminder of Mary's surprise visit from the angel Gabriel.

You will need:

✂

Colored cardstock or construction paper

Glue stick

Ruler, pencil, and scissors

Paints and brush

Prismatic stickers or holographic paper

Small length of gold cord or yarn and thread

1 Cut the cardstock in half. Fold one piece in half to make the card. It is easier to decorate the card before sticking in the pop-up, so paint a design on the back and front, or use stickers or holographic paper.

2 Use the pencil and ruler to draw a strip 6" x 1" long on the second piece of cardstock, then cut it out. Fold the strip exactly in half and crease the center fold. Make two more folds in the strip ¾" from each end as shown.

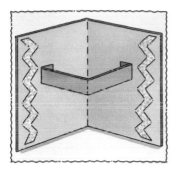

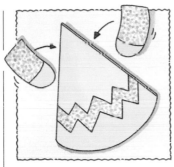

5 Cut out two wings from holographic paper and an oval shape from plain cardstock for the head. Draw the angel's face on the oval and glue it to the top of the body. Glue the wings to the back. To make the curly hair, take a 4" piece of gold cord or yarn. Tie it firmly in the center with thread and fray the ends. Glue the hair to the head.

3 Glue the strip in the middle of the card so the creases in the strip and the card match exactly. Keep the strip in this position and stick the two ends to the card with the glue stick.

4 Make your pop-up angel from scraps of paper as shown here. Cut out triangles and two arms from the scraps of cardstock. Cover these with small pieces of holographic paper to decorate the angel's robe. Glue the arms to the body.

6 When the glue is completely dry, fold the angel in half and make a firm crease along the center fold. Glue the angel to the pop-up strip, making sure the crease on the strip and the angel's fold match up exactly. When you open the card, the angel will pop out.

48

MARY AND JOSEPH TRAVEL TO BETHLEHEM

At last they could *see* the rooftops of Bethlehem!

Luke 2:1–5

1 Make the pockets by folding one of the long strips of felt in half lengthways and pinning together. Mark 12 pockets by drawing a line with the felt-tipped pen at 2" intervals along the strip.

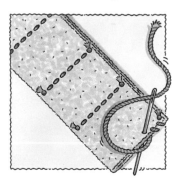

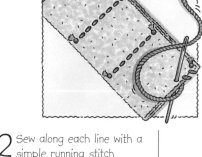

You will need:

Piece of blue felt, 24" x 16"

Pins, needle, and thread

Two strips of colored felt, 24" x 4"

Scissors

Pieces of colored felt: yellow, green, brown, gray, purple, etc.

Craft glue and spreader

Gold fabric marker

Ruler

Colored braid and sequins for decoration (optional)

Fine felt-tipped pen

Small toys and candy for each pocket

Four curtain rings

2 Sew along each line with a simple running stitch, knotting the thread at each end on the same side as the felt-tipped pen lines, making this side the back. Sew each end of the strip. Repeat with the other strip until all 24 pockets are done.

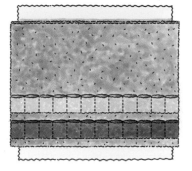

3 Spread craft glue along the back of the first strip of pockets and glue it to the bottom of the piece of blue felt. Then glue the second strip of pockets above the first. This leaves plenty of space above the pockets for the Bethlehem scene.

4 Cut out the shapes to make the city scene. The buildings are all rectangles. Start by gluing down the large shapes at the back of the town, but use the glue sparingly.

49

Mary waited several months before her baby was ready to be born. During that time, the Roman emperor ordered a census (which is a counting of all the people in the land). Joseph was told that he must go to Bethlehem to be counted. Mary and Joseph traveled all the way to Bethlehem. It was a very long, dusty journey. Mary would have been very tired. She was nearly ready to have her baby and needed to rest often.

Suddenly, over the brow of a hill, they were able to see the rooftops and trees of the little town of Bethlehem. At last they were nearly there!

Count the days to Christmas with this Advent calendar!

5 Build up the scene, working forward and overlapping the houses. Position the palm trees by gluing the trunks down first, then adding the leaves. Finally, cut out small yellow and orange squares and rectangles to make the lighted windows and doors.

6 Use the gold fabric marker to write the numbers 1 to 24 on each pocket. Add extra decorations and sequins if you have them. Sew the curtain rings along the top of calendar. Here's the fun part! Fill all the pockets with candy and small toys. Hang the calendar so it's ready for December 1.

BETHLEHEM IS FULL

Luke 2:1–7
No room at the inn!

When Mary and Joseph finally arrived in Bethlehem, they were very tired. They needed to find a place to sleep for the night. Mary's baby, who was God's Son, would be born soon!

Joseph knocked on the door of the inn, but it was already full. Many people had come to Bethlehem to be counted, just like Joseph. Now where could they stay?

The innkeeper said, "I'm sorry there's no room in my inn. But you are welcome to sleep in the place behind the inn where the animals stay. At least the straw is dry and you'll be safe for the night."

"Thank you!" said Joseph. Mary and Joseph followed the innkeeper behind the inn. At last Mary could lie down and rest.

You will need:

Rectangles of fabric or felt, about 10" x 5"

Scissors, needle, sewing thread, and pins

Craft glue, brush, and toothpicks as an alternative to sewing

Small scraps of colored fabric or felt for decoration

Lengths of colored cord or yarn, about 24" for each bag

Sequins for decoration

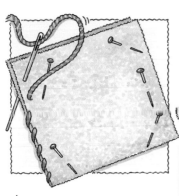

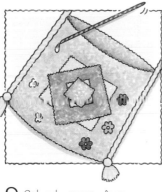

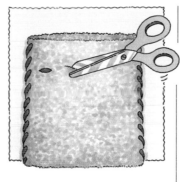

1 Fold the rectangle of fabric in half and pin the sides together. Sew along the two sides using small stitches and leave the top open. Or you can glue the two sides together with craft glue.

3 Cut out squares from different colored felt or fabric and glue them in patterns to both sides of the bag. Then sew or glue sequins to the bag to complete the design. Fill with small gifts or candy.

4 To make the drawstring bag, use the tips of the scissors to carefully snip a row of holes in the bag 1" from the top. Make the holes about ¾" apart and large enough to thread the cord or yarn through.

5 Take a 24" length of cord, tie knots approximately 1" from each end, and thread the cord in and out through the holes in the top of the bag.

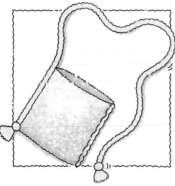

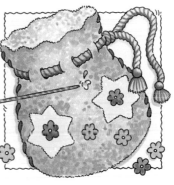

2 To make the bag with the long strap, take the 24" length of cord or yarn and tie a knot approximately 1" from each end to stop the cord from fraying. Then sew or glue the cord along both sides of the bag so the knots are positioned at the bottom corners of the bag.

6 Cut out some star shapes from colored felt and glue them around the bag. Then sew or glue sequins to the bag and around the opening. Fill the bag with candy or small toys to make really special Christmas gifts.

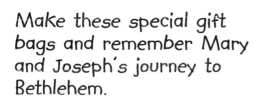

Make these special gift bags and remember Mary and Joseph's journey to Bethlehem.

JESUS IS BORN

Luke 2:6–7

Mary has a baby boy.

The time came for Mary's baby to be born.

"It's a boy!" shouted Joseph.

"He is named Jesus," said Mary. The angel Gabriel had told her to give Him that important name. "Jesus" means "the Lord saves."

Mary looked lovingly at her tiny first-born son. Mary knew that God had a very important plan for His Son. Jesus would be the Savior of the world! He would die for everyone's sins.

Mary wrapped her baby in cloths and laid Him in a manger to sleep.

Make these finger puppets to recreate the wonder of the Christmas story.

You will need:

Scraps of colored felt and fabric

Scissors and pins

Sewing needle and threads to match the felt

Craft glue, brush, and toothpicks

Beads and scraps of yarn to decorate the figures

1 Sketch patterns for Joseph, the shepherds, and Wise Men. You will need two body shapes, arms, and a headdress, face, and beard. Pin the two body pieces together and sew around the edge with small stitches, leaving the bottom open. (Option: Glue the body pieces together.)

2 Use a toothpick to glue all the other small pieces of felt to the body, dabbing small amounts of glue where it is needed. First glue the arms into position across the back.

3 The headdress is glued in place over the top of the body, then the face and beard. Finally, glue beads to the face, a small stick to a hand, and a small piece of thread around the head as a headband. Use different colored felt for all the men and decorate the Wise Men's clothes with beads.

5 To make the animals, use the photos here to guide you as you cut all the pieces you need. Pin and sew the body pieces together as before. To make the sheep, sew the nose to the face, glue two ears to the back of the face, then glue the face to the body

6 For the donkey and ox, glue nose shapes, ears, and eyes directly to the bodies. Make tails and manes from pieces of yarn which you can sew or glue in place.

4 To make Mary, follow the instructions for Joseph but use the needle and red thread to sew the nose and mouth features before gluing the face to the headdress. To make baby Jesus, use the smaller body shape.

54

Make these Christmas cards to give to your family and friends.

THE SHEPHERDS' SURPRISE

Luke 2:8–20

An angel told the shepherds some wonderful news.

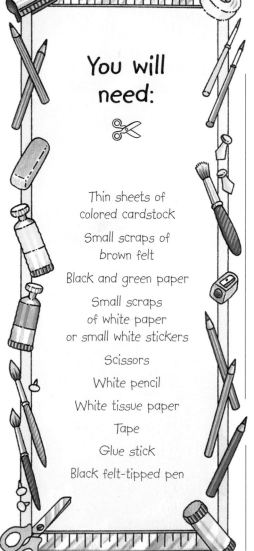

You will need:

✂

Thin sheets of colored cardstock

Small scraps of brown felt

Black and green paper

Small scraps of white paper or small white stickers

Scissors

White pencil

White tissue paper

Tape

Glue stick

Black felt-tipped pen

On the hills near Bethlehem, a group of shepherds were looking after their sheep. It was night and they had to make sure that no wild animals would come to snatch their sheep away.

Suddenly there was a blinding flash in the sky. An angel appeared!

"Don't be afraid!" he said. "I have come to bring you good news. This very night a baby has been born in Bethlehem. He is Christ the Lord! You will find the baby wrapped in strips of cloth and lying in a manger. Go now and see Him!"

The shepherds were so frightened and amazed that they could not speak.

Then a whole host of angels appeared in the sky, singing, "Glory to God in the highest, and on earth peace to all people in His favor!" It was a beautiful sound.

The shepherds left their sheep and hurried to Bethlehem, where they found the baby Jesus just as the angel had said.

When they left, they told everyone what they had seen and heard. They praised and thanked God for keeping His promise to send a Savior. That Savior, Jesus, was born for me and for you and for everyone.

1 Use the white pencil to draw a simple outline of a sheep on the black paper. Then cut it out carefully with scissors.

3 Tear up small pieces of white tissue paper, roll them into small balls with your fingers and glue them to the body of the sheep. Start around the edge, gluing small areas with the glue stick as you go. Gradually fill in the body shape leaving the black head and legs showing.

5 Cut a long grassy strip from the green paper and glue it along the bottom of the card. Cut out two white spots for eyes, or use white stickers, and glue them to the face. Make pupils with a black felt-tipped pen. You could also glue paper or attach stickers to the background as snowflakes.

2 To make the stand-up card, fold a sheet of cardstock in half and glue the sheep shape to the center of the card using the glue stick.

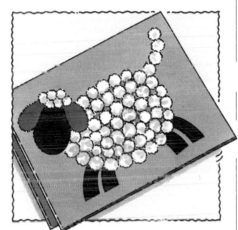

4 Cut out two ear shapes from the felt and glue them to the head. Glue more white tissue balls to the top of the head and also make a long curly white tail.

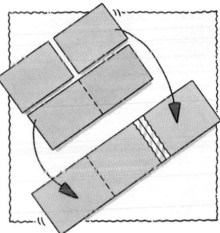

6 The zig-zag card is made in a similar way. Fold a sheet of cardstock into four as shown. Cut along the long center fold and across one of the pieces. Then tape the two pieces together as shown above. Decorate the card with three sheep

SHEPHERDS GO TO FIND JESUS

The baby in the manger.   Luke 2:16–20

"Hurry, hurry!" shouted the shepherds. "We must hurry to Bethlehem to find the baby God's angel has told us about!"

They hurried through the town, looking for a newborn baby. They knocked at the door of an inn.

"Is there a baby here?" they asked the innkeeper.

The innkeeper showed the shepherds where the animals stayed. Here they found Mary and Joseph and the baby just as the angels had said. In a manger, wrapped up in cloths, was the newborn baby: Jesus, their Savior. The shepherds looked at the tiny baby and they felt great joy.

When they had said good-bye, the shepherds hurried into the town telling everyone they met, "We've seen Him! We've seen Christ, the Lord!"

We can share this message too. We can tell people that Jesus is born. He saves us all from sin.

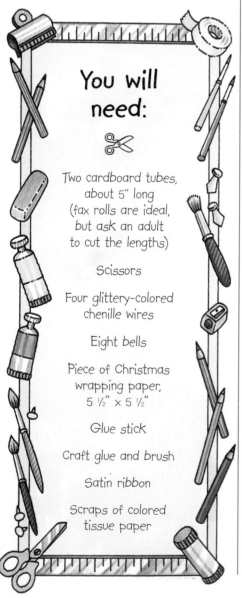

You will need:

✂

Two cardboard tubes, about 5" long (fax rolls are ideal, but ask an adult to cut the lengths)

Scissors

Four glittery-colored chenille wires

Eight bells

Piece of Christmas wrapping paper, 5 ½" x 5 ½"

Glue stick

Craft glue and brush

Satin ribbon

Scraps of colored tissue paper

1 Place the cardboard tube on top of the wrapping paper, leaving 1/4" of paper at either end. Use the glue stick to glue the paper to the tube and tuck the excess paper into the ends of the tube.

2 Twist two of the chenille wires together to join them and keep twisting for approximately 3". Then thread the first bell onto one chenille wire and twist both together as shown to hold the bell in place.

3 Continue twisting the chenille sticks, threading on four bells at equal distances apart. Finish twisting the last length together.

4 Dab a little craft glue onto the ends of the chenille wires, covering about 2" at both ends. Push the chenille wires into each end of the tube and allow to dry. If the cardboard tube is rather wide, fill any gaps with pieces of scrunched up tissue paper. Dabs of glue will hold it in place.

5 Finally, tie a length of ribbon around the chenille wires at either end of the tube, just where they are attached to the tube. Repeat these instructions to make the second set of Christmas bells. Now rejoice like the shepherds!

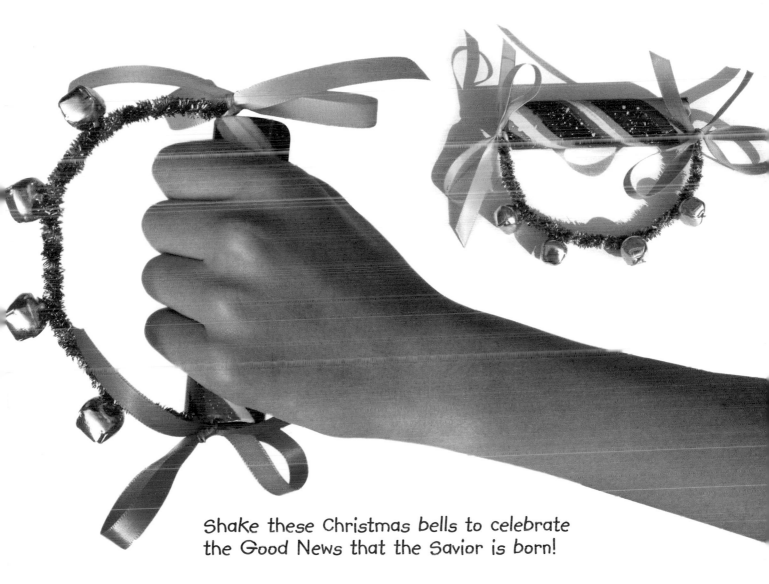

Shake these Christmas bells to celebrate the Good News that the Savior is born!

JESUS IS PRESENTED IN THE TEMPLE

A very special baby.

Luke 2:21–32

When Jesus was almost six weeks old, Mary and Joseph took Him to the temple in Jerusalem with two doves as their offering. They wanted to present Him to God and say thank You for their new son, as the Old Testament required.

In the temple there was a very old man called Simeon. He had been waiting all his life to see the Savior that God had promised to send. God had told Simeon that he would not die until he had seen the Messiah.

When Mary and Joseph came with Jesus, Simeon knew at once that this was the Child he had been waiting all his life to see. He took Jesus in his arms and praised the Lord.

"Lord God, now I may go in peace for I have seen the Savior, the one who will bring light to all the people of God."

We, too, can rejoice that Jesus came to earth. We can thank God for sending Jesus to bring us forgiveness and salvation.

You will need:

Three long craft chenille wires

Paper towels

Tape

Corrugated cardboard or foam core

Craft glue and brush

Craft Knife and cutting board

Gold poster paint and brush

Lid, about 3" in diameter

Newspaper

Red votive candle

Scraps of garland and ribbon for decoration

Some adult help with using the craft knife and lighting the candle

SAFETY NOTE:
This project is designed to be used as a table decoration. The candle should always be lit by an adult and should never be left unattended.

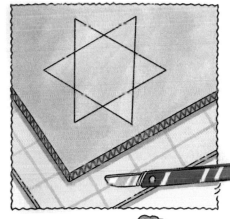

1 Take each chenille wire and bend both ends into a curly shape. Then firmly twist all the chenille wires together in the center so they hold together and make the legs for the candle holder.

Make this beautiful candle holder to remind you that Jesus is the Light of the world.

2 Draw a large star on the corrugated cardboard or foam core by drawing two overlapping triangles. Ask an adult to help cut out the star with the craft knife.

3 Cover the chenille wires completely with several layers of glued strips of paper towel. This can get messy, so cover the surface you are using with plenty of newspaper. Use the glue sparingly and let it dry between layers.

4 Cover one side of the star with glued paper towel to give it a textured finish. Leave it to dry, then cover the other side.

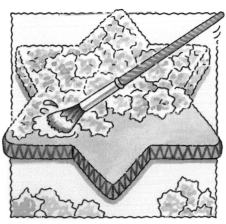

5 Place the star on a flat surface and position the chenille wires on top. Hold them in place with tape and continue to apply glued paper towel to secure the chenille wire legs firmly to the star. When the legs are dry, they should be perfectly rigid and should support the star when turned right-side up.

6 Glue the lid to the center of the star and cover with the glued paper towel. When you are happy that the candle holder is completely covered with the textured effect, allow it to dry and paint it gold. Place the candle in the holder and wrap a small piece of tinsel, ribbon, or other small decorations around the center of the holder.

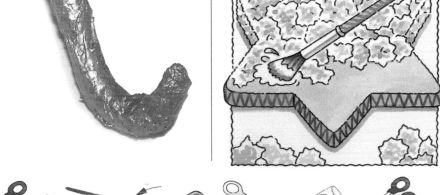

A NEW STAR IN THE SKY

Matthew 2:1–2
The journey of the Wise Men.

When Jesus was born, some Wise Men in the East were looking at the stars. They noticed a very bright new star in the sky and were very excited.

"Look at that!" said one of the Wise Men. "The new King must have been born! We will go to worship Him."

So the Wise Men set off to follow the star. They took with them fine gifts for the new King.

They followed the star by day and by night, over deserts and hills. God was leading the Wise Men to find Jesus.

To make the wrapping paper: Draw stars with a black felt-tipped pen on a sheet of white paper. When you place the tissue paper over the stars, you will be able to see the outlines through the tissue.

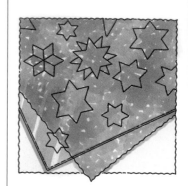

You will need:

Pack of colored tissue paper
or
colored hand-made papers

Gold or silver fabric paint

Gold felt-tipped pen or glitter pens

Construction paper

Scissors

Glue stick

Black felt-tipped pen and white paper (optional)

Use this star wrapping paper to wrap up your Christmas gifts.

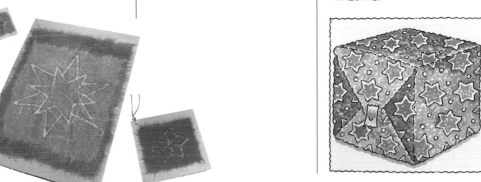

2 Carefully trace the stars onto the tissue paper with the gold pen or fabric paint. Trace as many stars as you can, drawing them all over the sheet. Draw a few test stars to see how long they take to dry. The paint must dry before moving the paper, otherwise the stars will smudge!

4 Overlap several pieces of tissue paper to make your design. The papers are very thin, so colors underneath will show through. Draw patterns and squiggles on the card with the gold pen to complete the design.

3 To make a Christmas card: Fold a piece of construction paper in half. Tear the tissue paper around the star designs, leaving the uneven torn edges. Glue the back of the paper stars with the glue stick and stick them to the card. The paper is very delicate, so use the glue stick carefully.

5 To make a gift tag: Cut out small tag-size cards and decorate as before.

6 When wrapping gifts using the star paper, you may need to wrap the present in plain paper first. The tissue paper is very thin and see-through, and you don't want to give away any secrets before Christmas!

You will need:

✂

Adult help in preparing and baking the cookies

Preheat oven to 350°F

4 oz. butter

10 oz. plain flour

4 oz. brown sugar

1 teaspoon baking powder

3 oz. corn syrup

2 teaspoons ground ginger

1 medium egg

1 teaspoon cinnamon

4 oz. sifted powdered sugar

1 tablespoon water

Food coloring, silver balls, and ribbon or cord for decoration

Wooden spoon and mixing bowl

Rolling pin

Greased baking sheet

Wire cooling rack

Dessert spoon

Cookie cutters

Drinking straw

GIFTS FOR THE BABY KING

Wise Men worship Jesus.

Matthew 2:9–12

The Wise Men set off toward Bethlehem. They followed the star to a small house in the town.

There they found Jesus and Mary. The Wise Men were overjoyed to find the baby King.

They bowed down low and worshiped Jesus.

They gave Him their fine gifts of gold, frankincense, and myrrh. Mary watched in wonder.

That night God came to the Wise Men in a dream and warned them not to return to Herod's palace. So the Wise Men returned to their homes by another route.

God led the Wise Men to Jesus with a bright star. Jesus was born for all people everywhere. He came at Christmas as a baby, and He comes today in His Word and in the Sacraments.

Make these delicious cookies to share at Christmas.

1 Cream the butter and sugar together in a bowl using the wooden spoon. Add the corn syrup and the egg, and mix until smooth.

2 Sift the flour, baking powder, and spices. Fold them into the mixture to form a stiff dough. Shape the dough into a ball and leave it in a cool place or the fridge for at least 1 hour.

3 Turn the dough onto a floured surface and roll out to ¼" thick. Use the cookie cutters to cut out shapes. Use the drinking straw to make a hole in some of the cookies to hang on the Christmas tree. This recipe will make approximately 8 large cookies and 20 small ones.

4 Place the cookies on a greased baking sheet and ask an adult to put them in a preheated oven to bake for 10-12 minutes or until light golden brown. Place on a wire rack to cool.

5 To make the icing, slowly stir the water into the powdered sugar until the icing is smooth and firm. If you want colored icing, add a few drops of food coloring.

6 Decorate the cookies with the icing and allow to dry. Thread ribbon through the holes of some of the cookies and hang them on the tree. The other cookies can be wrapped and given as Christmas presents or shared with visitors.

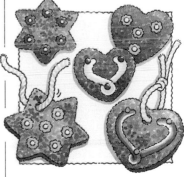

64

Luke 1:26–2:20; Matthew 2:1–12

THE CHRISTMAS STORY

Angels, shepherds, and Wise Men welcome Jesus, our Savior.

God sent an angel to tell Mary that she would have a baby called Jesus, who would be the Son of God.

Mary and Joseph traveled to Bethlehem, where Jesus was born. Mary laid her new baby in a manger on the soft hay.

God sent angels to tell some shepherds near Bethlehem the good news: "Go and find the baby Jesus."

The sky was bright with dazzling light and a song rang 'round the hills: "Glory to God in the highest!"

When the shepherds reached the town, they found Jesus and worshiped Him. They left filled with joy, eager to tell others all they had seen and heard.

Later, Wise Men came from faraway lands to visit Jesus. They followed a very bright star in the sky. When they found Jesus, they gave Him gifts of gold, frankincense, and myrrh. At last they had found the baby King, born to be the Savior of all!

You will need:

✂

White pencil

Dark colored cardstock, construction paper, or craft foam sheets

Scissors

Hole punch

Clear colored candy wrappers

Glue stick

Gold thread

Large blunt needle

1 Use the white pencil to draw a simple animal shape on the cardstock. Then cut out the shape.

2 Draw star shapes on the animal and carefully cut them out.

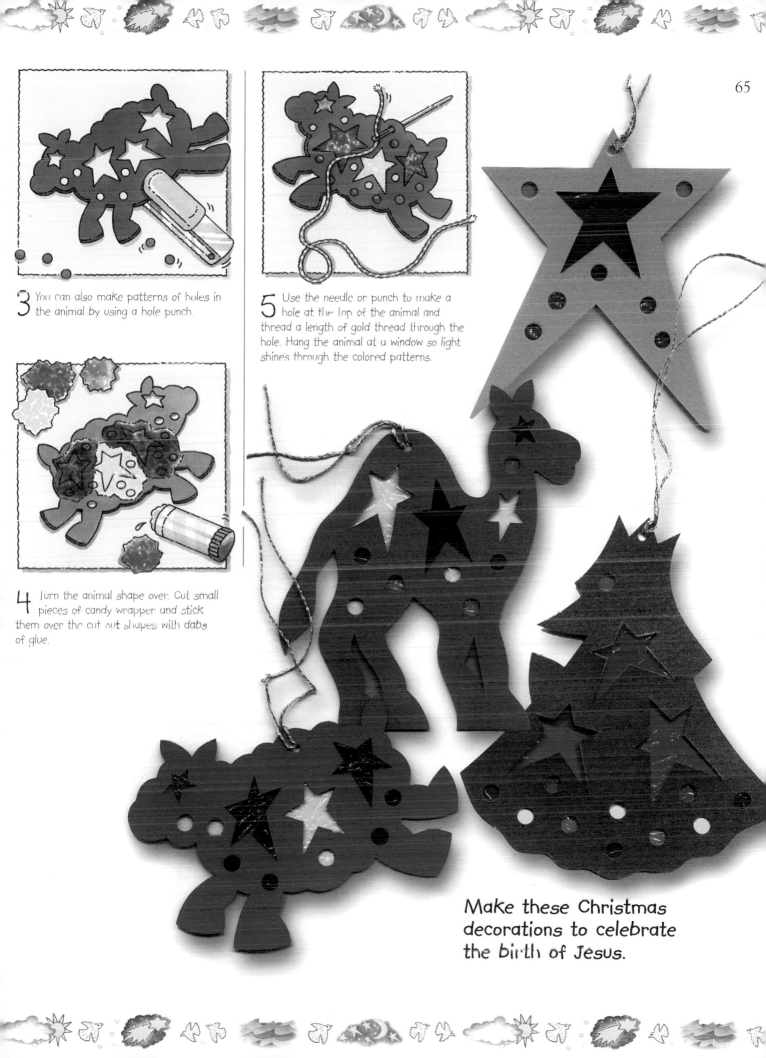

3 You can also make patterns of holes in the animal by using a hole punch.

5 Use the needle or punch to make a hole at the top of the animal and thread a length of gold thread through the hole. Hang the animal at a window so light shines through the colored patterns.

4 Turn the animal shape over. Cut small pieces of candy wrapper and stick them over the cut out shapes with dabs of glue.

Make these Christmas decorations to celebrate the birth of Jesus.

66

JESUS IS BAPTIZED

John baptized Jesus in the Jordan River.

There was a man called John the Baptizer who told the people the Savior was coming. He told them to turn away from their sins and be sorry for the wrong things they had done. Many people believed John's words and were baptized.

One day, Jesus came to the river to see John.

"I want you to baptize Me in the river," said Jesus.

John was very surprised. He knew that Jesus had come to save all people from sin.

John agreed to baptize Jesus. When he finished, as Jesus was praying, the Holy Spirit came down from heaven in the shape of a dove. And then God the Father's voice said, "This is My Son whom I love, with Him I am pleased."

Jesus really was God's promised Savior.

You will need:

✂

Light-colored cardstock
Dark-colored cardstock
Pencil
Scissors
Craft knife and cutting mat
Glue stick
Sequins
Felt-tipped pens
Elastic

1 Draw a simple dove shape on the light cardstock and cut it out carefully.

2 Draw a wing shape on the light cardstock, cut it out and use it as a pattern to make two more shapes for the second wing and the tail.

3 Decorate the wings and the tail with feather shapes cut from dark cardstock and decorate with sequins. Glue them in place with the glue stick.

4 Ask an adult to cut slots in the middle of the dove's body and by the tail with the craft knife. Decorate both sides of the body with sequins.

5 Cut a strip of light cardstock wide enough to fit through the center slot and glue a wing to each end of the strip. Make a small cut in the tail shape and slide it into the body.

Make this dove and hang it near a window.

6 Use the felt-tipped pens to color in the dove's beak and eyes or glue a triangle of dark cardstock over the beak area. Make a small hole in the top of the dove where marked, thread through a length of elastic, tying it firmly, and hang.

The Temptation of Jesus

Jesus stayed in the wilderness for 40 days and nights.

After Jesus was baptized, He went into the wilderness and ate nothing for forty days and nights. When He was very hungry, the devil came and tempted Him to misuse His power.

First, the devil tried to persuade Jesus to turn stones into bread to ease His hunger. Second, Jesus was taken to the top of the temple and told to jump off so the angels would catch Him. Lastly, the devil offered Jesus kingship over all the earth if He would only bow down and worship him. But Jesus did not give in to temptation. He used passages from Scripture to show the devil he was wrong to tempt Him.

You will need:

✂

Empty potato chip can with plastic lid

Craft knife (and some adult help)

Craft paints and brush

Pencil

Green construction paper

Circle of blue paper (optional)

Scissors

3 chenille wires

Craft glue in bottle with nozzle

Brown yarn

1 Turn the can upside-down so the plastic lid becomes the base. Ask an adult to help you make the slot near the top of the can using the craft knife. Make the slot big enough to take coins.

3 To make the palm trees that decorate the box, first cut out the palm leaves. You can draw them free-hand and cut six leaves for each tree.

2 Paint the box with a desert scene of blue sky and golden sand dunes. Paint the top of the box, or glue on a circle of blue paper.

4 Position the 6 leaves together in a bunch as shown. Fold a chenille wire in half and twist it around the stem to secure the leaves. Continue twisting the chenille wire to make the tree trunk.

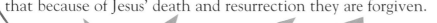

Many Christians use the forty days of Lent to remember Jesus' temptation in the wilderness. They think about sin and their need for a Savior. The day before Lent is called Shrove Tuesday. Years ago people would go to the priest to confess the wrong things they had done so they could be forgiven. Today some people make pancakes as a last big meal before remembering Jesus' time of fasting. Some give up a favorite food or a bad habit during Lent.

On Ash Wednesday the palms saved from the previous year's Palm Sunday can be burned and used in a special church service. In some churches, the pastor marks the sign of the cross with some of the ash on each person's forehead to show that because of Jesus' death and resurrection they are forgiven.

Make this bank to help save money during Lent, and give the money as an offering in church.

5 Cover the chenille wire with brown yarn by wrapping it around the trunk and gluing it in place.

6 Make two more palm trees and glue them in place around the bank. It may help to glue one palm tree at a time, letting it dry before gluing the others in place. Use the bank to save money during Lent so you can give it as an offering. Empty the bank by carefully removing the plastic lid at the base.

John 2:1–11

THE WEDDING AT CANA

Jesus turned water into wine!

Jesus was once a guest at a wedding in Cana. There was a great feast and everyone was enjoying the party when suddenly the wine began to run out.

"You must do something," said Mary, Jesus' mother. But Jesus knew what God wanted Him to do.

He told the servants to fill six large stone jars with water, then take them to the man in charge of the feast. When the man tasted it, he was very pleased.

You will need:

✂

Heavy, flexible cardboard

Pencil and ruler

Craft knife and cutting board

Four toothpicks

Small bells, metal buttons, washers, keys

Jingles and beads

Tape

Craft glue, brush, and small bowl

Newspaper

Poster paints and brushes

Tacky Glue®

Ribbons for decoration

Varnish

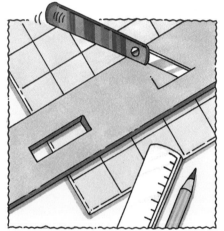

1 With an adult's help, use the craft knife and cutting board to cut a length of cardboard approximately 3½" x 16". Mark four evenly spaced holes on the cardboard with a pencil and cut them out.

2 Make jingles from any metal objects such as buttons, washers, keys, and bells. Thread them onto toothpicks separated with beads and hold in place with Tacky Glue®.

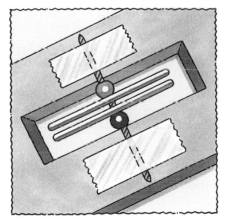

"Usually people serve the best wine first," the man said, "but you have left the best wine till last!" He didn't know that Jesus had done a miracle.

Jesus had turned the water into wine. He revealed His great power as God's Son.

Jesus cares for us too. He helps us in all our troubles. We can rejoice that Jesus is true God and true man.

Make this tambourine and imagine you are dancing at a wedding feast.

3 Place each threaded stick over a hole, being careful not to dislodge the beads and jingles. Tape them securely.

4 Bend the cardboard into a circle and tape the ends together. Then cover the cardboard with pieces of newspaper soaked in glue.

5 Cover the whole tambourine with several layers of glued paper to strengthen it. Make sure you glue around the holes neatly with smaller pieces of newspaper.

6 Leave the tambourine to completely dry before painting. Decorate with bright-colored patterns and when the paint is dry, give it a coat of varnish. Finally, thread ribbon through the holes and tie on extra bells if you have them.

THE CENTURION'S FAITH

Luke 7:1–10

A Roman officer asks for help from Jesus.

Jesus healed many people so crowds often followed Him.

One day a Roman officer begged Jesus for help.

"My servant is very ill and cannot move."

Jesus replied, "I will go and make him well."

"No, no," said the officer. "I know that if You just say the word, he will be healed. I trust that You will heal him."

Jesus was pleased to hear that the officer trusted Him.

"Go home, then," said Jesus. "What you believe will be done."

The officer ran home and found to his great joy that Jesus had healed his servant.

We have great joy too because all our sins are forgiven through Jesus. We have new life in Him.

Make this Roman army helmet, similar to that worn by the Roman officer.

To make the helmet, glue torn pieces of newspaper over the top half of the balloon using the craft glue. Cover the balloon with three more layers. Allow glue to dry completely.

You will need:

✂

Blown-up balloon

Newspaper

Craft glue and brush

Thin cardstock

Scissors

Plastic bowl

Silver and black poster paints

Paint brush

Sharp pencil

Thick string or cord

Brads

2 Pop the balloon and remove it. Cut off the uneven edge of paper. You will now have the shape that forms the top part of the helmet.

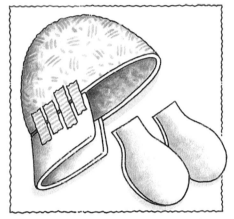

3 Cut out a collar and two ear flaps from the cardstock. The collar will be attached to the back of the helmet and the ear flaps will be attached to the sides. Attach with glued strips of paper.

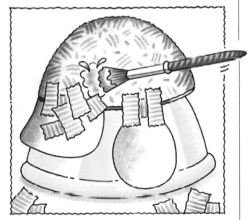

4 Support the helmet over a plastic bowl while you work. Cover the helmet and card shapes with three more layers of glued newspaper pieces, then leave to dry.

5 Wind and glue a length of string around the brim of the helmet. Attach brads to look like rivets. To attach the brads, first make a hole in the helmet with a sharp pencil. Push the brad through and cover the splayed ends with pieces of glued newspaper.

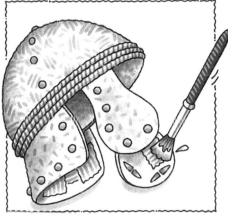

6 Paint the helmet with silver poster paint, making sure that the paint covers all the string and paper. To give the helmet a tarnished metallic look, mix some black paint with the silver and brush this sparingly over the silver surface. You could also paint the inside of the helmet black. Make sure the paint is dry before trying it on!

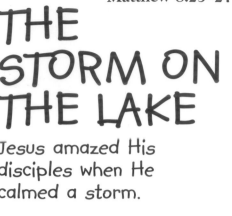

Matthew 8:23–27

THE STORM ON THE LAKE

Jesus amazed His disciples when He calmed a storm.

Jesus and His friends were in a boat on the lake when a fierce storm blew up and the boat was tossed about like a cork.

Jesus was fast asleep in the boat, but His disciples were terrified of sinking.

"Save us, Lord!" they shouted to Jesus.

"Why are you so afraid?" said Jesus. Then He got up and ordered the wind and the waves to calm down.

The storm vanished. Everyone was amazed!

"Even the winds and the waves obey Him!" they said.

Jesus saved His friends from the storm. We, too, ask Jesus to help us in all our troubles. He is with those who call on Him.

Make this simple fishing boat and think about Jesus' power over all creation.

1 Paint the 12" x 8" card to look like the wooden hull of a boat and let it dry. Fold the card in half lengthways. Draw an angle at each end and trim with scissors.

You will need:

12" x 8" piece and several scraps of stiff, brown cardstock

Paints and brush

Scissors

Craft glue and brush

Craft knife and cutting board

Pencil and ruler

String for rigging

Square of fabric, 8" x 8"

Two 10" dowels

Scraps of netting and shiny paper fishes

Brad

Narrow strip of cardstock, folded into a zigzag shape, with slots cut into it

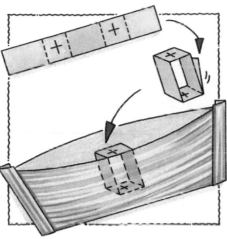

2 Cut two lengths of card 1½" wide and 5" long. Paint them to look like wood and let dry. Fold each piece in half lengthways and glue to each end of the hull.

3 To make the mast support, cut a strip of card 1" x 8" and divide it into sections as shown. Cut an "X" in the two shorter sections with the craft knife and fold the strip along the dotted line to make a square. Glue or tape the support to the center of the hull.

5 Loosely roll up the sail and tie it to the top of the mast. Then put the mast into the slot in the mast support.

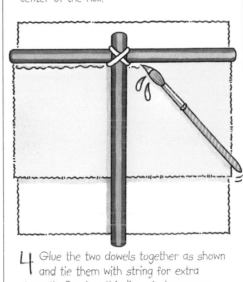

4 Glue the two dowels together as shown and tie them with string for extra strength. Brush a thin line of glue across the top of the sail fabric, place it on the horizontal dowel, and let dry.

6 Cut out a rudder shape from the cardstock and paint it to look like wood. Attach it to the side of the boat with a brad. To make the boat look more realistic, use the string to add extra rigging. If you use netting, drape it over the side with a full catch of paper fish!

Note: Because the boat does not have a flat bottom, it will need to be propped up or slotted into a zigzag shape of stiff cardstock. Cut four slots to stand the boat up as shown in the photograph.

76

LOAVES AND FISHES
Jesus feeds more than five thousand people!

Large crowds followed Jesus because they had heard of His miraculous deeds. There were men, women, and even children. They had been listening to Him all day and were getting hungry.

Jesus' friends thought the people should go away and buy some food, but Jesus wanted to feed them.

"What food have you got?" He asked His friends.

"Only five loaves and two fishes," they replied.

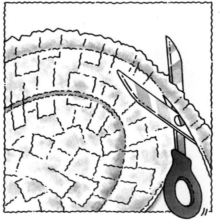

Jesus then did something amazing—a miracle! He gave thanks and shared the food among all 5,000 people! No one went away hungry.

Jesus provides us today with all that we have. He takes care of our bodies and souls.

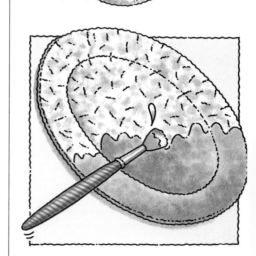

1 Use the plate as a mold. Lightly grease the plate with cooking oil and cover with plastic wrap. Then cover the plate with six layers of newspaper strips, glued with diluted glue. This will form the plaque for your mosaic.

You will need:
✂

Oval plastic plate

Newspaper

Gray paint and paint brush

Pencil

Spray shellac

Cooking oil and plastic wrap

Craft glue and brush

Scissors

Colored magazine pictures or gift wrap

2 Leave the paper plaque to dry overnight, then remove it from the plate by pulling away the plastic wrap. Neaten the plaque by trimming around the edge with scissors.

3 Choose a neutral gray color to paint the plaque. This will be the base color of your mosaic.

This beautiful mosaic fish will remind you of how Jesus fed the people.

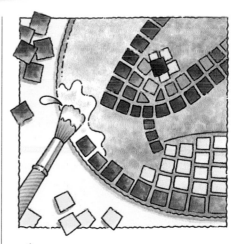

4 Sketch the outline of a fish onto the plaque with a pencil. Add in details like the eye, fins, and tail, and make a border round the edge of the plaque.

5 Cut out squares of colored paper. Arrange the squares into groups of similar colors.

6 Follow the pencil lines of the fish, and glue the squares to the plaque. Build up the mosaic pattern, overlapping the squares if necessary. Finally, spray the finished plaque with shellac to strengthen and protect the mosaic.

THE GOOD SEED

Luke 8:5–15   Jesus told this parable to a large crowd beside the Sea of Galilee.

"Listen! There was once a man who went to sow some seed.

Some of the seed fell along the path where birds came and ate it.

Some of the seed fell on rocky ground where it could not grow.

Some of the seed fell among thorn bushes, which choked the young plants.

But some of the seed fell in good soil. The plants grew and produced a good harvest."

What did the story mean?

God is the sower. The seed is His message. Some people hear God's message but forget about Him. Some people try to follow God but give up when trouble comes their way. Some people become too busy with worries, money, and other things.

But other people are like the seed in good soil; they hear God's message, follow God, and live for Him. God gives the seed and the growth.

You will need:

✄

Pencil

Sheet of colored, heavy cardstock

Scissors

Craft glue
(in a plastic bottle with a tip)

Glue spreader or brush

Collage materials:
dried seeds, beans, lentils, split peas

Dried grasses or stems of wheat

1 First you will need to sketch out the design of the collage on the colored card. Draw the outline of the bird flying over the cornfield. Draw a patterned border around the edge of the card.

2 If you need to, use the scissors to trim the cardstock to the correct size for your design. This will give you guidelines when you start assembling the collage.

3 Begin with the main shapes. Spread the glue along the outline of the bird and press the beans into the glue. Work around the edge of the flying bird first and then fill in the rest of the body.

Make this beautiful collage using dried seeds and grasses.

4 Spread glue carefully over the bottom section of the background which shows the cornfield. Glue the dried grasses and stems of wheat in place.

5 Spread a thin line of glue along the edges of the collage and press a row of beans into the glue to make the border. Put small blobs of glue over the background sky and glue small seeds in place. The glue will dry clear so it won't show when your collage is finished.

HIDDEN TREASURE

Matthew 13:44

The parable of the hidden treasure.

Jesus told this story about the great value of the kingdom of heaven:

"A man found some treasure hidden in a field. It was beautiful! It sparkled in the sunlight and the man wanted to keep it.

He sold everything he had. With the money he got, he bought the field with the treasure in it. Now the treasure belonged to him! He was really happy!"

Jesus often told people parables like this to teach His followers more about the kingdom of God and how valuable it is. He wanted others to think about the precious kingdom where Christ the Savior rules with the Gospel. Jesus told them that, like the hidden treasure in the field, being God's child in Christ is worth more than anything else in the world.

You will need:

✂

Cardboard box with an attached lid

Sheet of heavy cardstock

Ruler, pencil, and scissors

Tape

Paper towels

Craft glue and brush

Lengths of yarn or string

Gold poster paint and brush

Selection of buttons, beads, pasta shapes, and plastic jewels

Toothpicks

4 small bottle tops (for the legs)

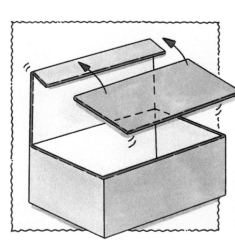

I Use the ruler and pencil to measure a 1" strip along the lid of the box and fold this over. Measure the top of the lid and cut a piece the same size from the cardstock. Tape it to the fold along the long sides.

Make this treasure chest to remind you of the man who bought the field.

3 Brush glue over a small part of the box. Tear up small pieces of paper towel and stick them to the surface. Make sure the glued paper stays nice and crinkly. Continue to glue the paper towel over the entire surface of the box and legs.

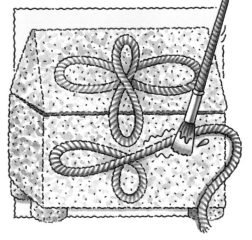

5 Glue yarn or string onto the box in curly patterns. Make an extra long loop on the lid and thread a large bead through the center of the chest to make the fastening. Also glue string around the rim of the open box. Don't worry if the glue looks a bit messy—you won't see it after the chest is painted!

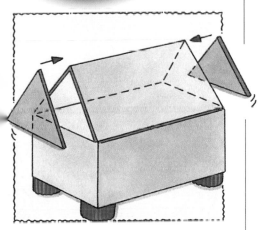

4 Glue a layer of paper over the hinge of the lid, but be careful not to glue the lid to the box — put a couple of tooth-picks across the opening to keep it apart. Leave the box to dry and then glue a layer of paper on the inside.

2 Measure two triangles of cardstock to fit exactly at each end of the lid. Cut them out and tape them to both ends of the lid to make the chest's new shaped lid. Glue four bottle tops to the base to make the chest's legs and stand the chest on the legs until they have stuck firmly.

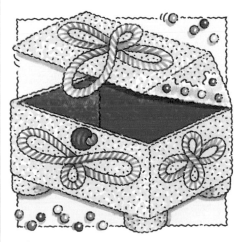

6 If you have buttons or pasta shapes to use as decoration, glue them to the chest before painting it. Then paint the chest in gold paint. Finally, glue on any colorful "jewels" and beads to make the treasure chest really sparkle!

82

THE WISE AND FOOLISH GIRLS

Matthew 25:1–13

Five girls were ready for the wedding, but five were not!

You will need:

✂

Self-hardening clay

Tea light candle

Plastic carving tools and plastic knife to shape the clay

Small sponge and water

Paints and spray shellac

Jesus once told a parable about ten girls at a wedding to explain what the kingdom of heaven will be like:

"There were once ten girls who were supposed to meet the bridegroom on his way to the wedding. They carried oil lamps to light the way. But the oil didn't last long in the lamps.

Five of the girls remembered to bring some extra oil with them. But the other five had forgotten. Their lamps went out and they had to run off to buy some more.

While they were away, the bridegroom arrived. The five girls whose lamps were burning brightly met him and went with him to the wedding. The door was shut.

When the other five girls finally arrived, they were too late for the wedding!"

Jesus told this parable to remind us that He is coming back; but since we don't know exactly when, we must always be ready for Him.

Take a piece of self-hardening clay and knead it in your hands until it is soft. Make a circle of clay roughly ½" thick and 3½" across. This will be the base of the lamp.

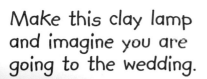

Make this clay lamp and imagine you are going to the wedding.

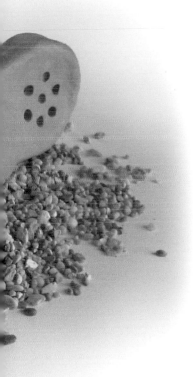

3 Mold the shape of the lamp with your fingers. If you need to, moisten the surface of the clay with a damp sponge to make it easier to work and shape.

5 Continue to smooth the sides and top of the lamp, using your fingers. Make the shape of a spout by pinching in the end of the lamp opposite the handle. Keeping the clay damp makes it easier to smooth the surface.

2 Place the tea light in the center of the base, keeping the candle in place in the center. Use small pieces of clay to build up the sides of the lamp.

SAFETY NOTE:

The clay lamp is designed to hold a tea light in a safe way—BUT it should not be lit without adult supervision or left unattended

4 Make a handle for the lamp from a piece of clay. Dampen the side of the lamp and attach the handle, then smooth over the joints with the tools and the damp sponge.

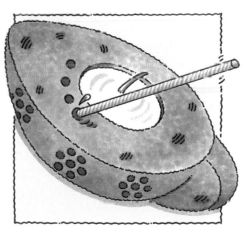

6 Make some simple patterns on the lamp using the tools, then allow it to dry. The lamp can be left in its natural clay finish, or it could be painted and sprayed with shellac.

THE LOST COIN

Luke 15:8–10

Jesus told this parable to show how people are special to God.

You will need:

✂

Compass
Pencil
Ruler
Cardstock
Scissors
Craft glue and brush
Lengths of colored cord or yarn
Single hole punch
Large blunt needle
Silver poster paint and brush
Dried beans, pasta, and sunflower seeds for decoration

Make this coin necklace with card medallions.

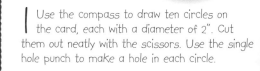

1 Use the compass to draw ten circles on the card, each with a diameter of 2". Cut them out neatly with the scissors. Use the single hole punch to make a hole in each circle.

2 Brush glue onto each circle and add the dried beans, seeds, and pasta to make patterns in the center of each circle. These shapes will make an attractive raised design on each coin, so don't worry about extra blobs of glue!

Jesus told this parable to explain why He accepted and recognized sinners. A woman had ten silver coins. She lost one and tried hard to find it. She lit a lamp, swept her house, and looked everywhere for it. Suddenly she found it! There it was, glinting in the sunlight.

The woman called her friends and neighbors and said, "Let's have a party! I am so happy to have found my lost coin!"

In the same way, there is rejoicing in heaven over one sinner who repents. Each person in God's kingdom is a precious treasure.

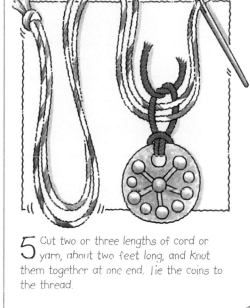

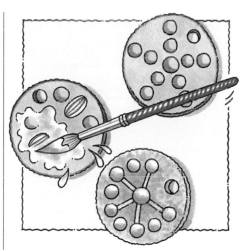

3 When all the textures are firmly glued in place and the glue is dry, paint the coins on both sides with silver poster paint and let dry.

5 Cut two or three lengths of cord or yarn, about two feet long, and knot them together at one end. Tie the coins to the thread.

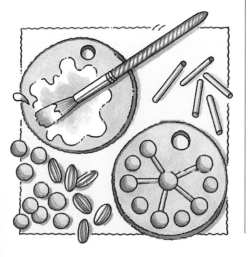

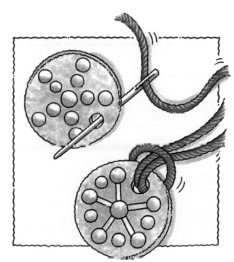

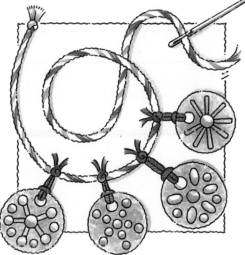

4 Thread the needle with 5" of cord or yarn. Pass it through the hole in the first coin and loop the thread around the hole. Then repeat this for all ten coins.

6 Place the finished necklace around your neck, tie the two ends together, and cut off any extra lengths. You could experiment by making other necklaces or bracelets with lots more coins decorated with different textures and colors.

JESUS ENTERS JERUSALEM

Matthew 21:1–1

You will need:

✂

Lengths of fabric approx. 8" wide

Craft glue and brush

Pins, sewing needle, and thread

Paints and brush

Small scraps of multicolored fabric or felt

Colored tape

2 dowels or bamboo canes

Wood balls or large beads

Trimmings—buttons and beads

Scissors

Colored yarn, cardstock, and scissors for tassel making

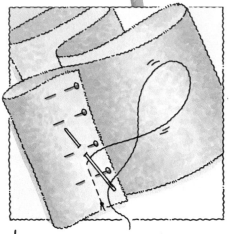

1 Cut a long length of fabric 8" wide. You can make the banner as long as you like! Turn a 1" strip of fabric over at each end, pin in place, and sew to form a casing for the dowels.

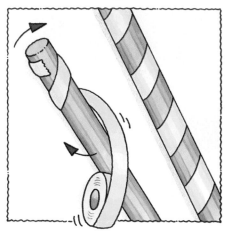

2 Give each dowel a coat of paint and allow to dry. Attach the colored tape to the top of the dowel, then slowly twist the dowel, sticking the tape firmly as it's turning. This gives the dowels an attractive diagonal pattern.

Crowds of people waved
palm branches to welcome the King!

Clip, clop went the donkey's hooves on the road.

"Hosanna! Hurray!" shouted the crowd.

Who was this riding on a donkey? It was Jesus!

The people were so excited to see this King, the Messiah.

They threw down cloaks in front of the donkey and waved palm branches in the air.

Later that week, Jesus would suffer and die for the sins of all. He truly is our Savior King!

Make this simple banner to praise and worship Jesus.

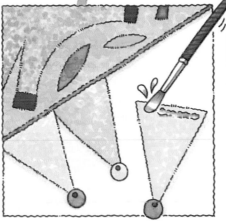

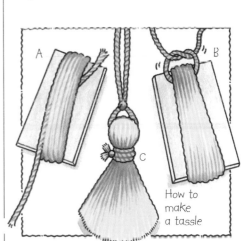

3 Use the fabric scraps to decorate the banner. Cut out flowers and animal shapes and arrange them along the length of fabric. Glue shapes in place when you are happy with your design.

4 Use the trimmings you have to make your banner as colorful as you wish. Sew or glue buttons and beads to the design, and attach a fringe or trim to the bottom edge.

5 Brush a small amount of glue onto the dowels, covering about 6" from the top, then carefully push them into the casing at each end of the banner. When the glue is dry, glue the wood balls or beads to the top of each dowel.

How to make a tassle

6 To make a tassel, wind yarn around a piece of cardstock (A). Tie the yarn together at the top and remove the card (B). Wind yarn around the top of the tassel, tie, then cut through the ends (C). Attach tassels to lengths of yarn and tie to the dowels.

88

JESUS CLEARS THE TEMPLE

Jesus takes action!

Matthew 21:12–13; Mark 11:15–18; Luke 19:45–47

While Jesus was in Jerusalem, He went to the temple. God's house was a place to pray in this noisy, bustling city.

But when Jesus entered the temple courtyard, He saw people buying and selling animals and doves, and other people cheating as they changed money. The temple had become a noisy, smelly market place, just like the rest of the city.

Jesus took action. He drove out the money changers and turned over the tables.

"You are turning My house into a den of robbers!" shouted Jesus. "It should be a house of prayer for all people!"

You will need:

✂

A small round wooden or cardboard box

Scissors
(and some adult help)

Ruler

16" x 1½"
balsa wood strip

Poster or craft paints
and brush

7 lengths of string,
cord, or yarn

Tapestry needle

3 large
wooden beads

1 Ask an adult to help you make three equally spaced holes in the rims of the lid and bottom of the round box, using the sharp point of the scissors.

2 Using the ruler to position them accurately, ask an adult to help you make three holes in the balsa wood strip, again using the point of the scissors. Make a hole exactly in the center of the strip and one hole 1" from each end.

Jesus wanted people to keep the temple a holy place. Jesus' actions and words made some people afraid and angry. The chief priests and teachers of the law saw Jesus as a threat and began to make plans to kill Him. But although leaders plotted against Jesus, He kept doing His Father's will.

Make scales like the money lenders used in the temple courts

3 Paint the lid and base of the box and the balsa wood strip. Money lenders' scales would have been made from metal, but you can paint your scales with bright colors and patterns.

4 Thread a length of string through each of the three holes in the lid of the box and tie a knot at the end of each string. Use the tapestry needle to thread the three strings through the hole in the end of the strip. Thread the strings through a bead, then tie the ends together.

5 Do the same thing to attach the base of the box to the other end of the strip. Thread the needle with the last piece of string and tie a knot in the end of the string. Thread it through a bead, then through the center hole, and tie a loop in the end.

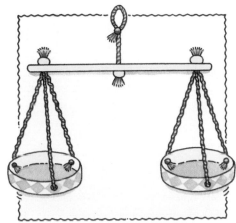

6 If you have measured the string equally and made your scales accurately, they should be evenly balanced when you hold them up by the center string. Use small coins as weights and use your scales to weigh small pieces of fruit, nuts, or candy.

JESUS IS ANOINTED
The smell of perfume fills the room.

Matthew 26:6–13; Mark 14:3–9

Shortly before Passover, Jesus went to eat at a friend's house. A woman named Mary came up to Jesus, holding a small but very precious alabaster jar.

When Mary opened the jar, the sweet smell of perfume wafted out. Mary had brought a very expensive gift for Jesus. To show her devotion for Jesus, she poured it over His head. This custom was common at feasts and was called "anointing."

"What's she doing?" asked some of Jesus' disciples. "That's a waste of money, just pouring it away like that!"

Jesus heard them complaining and said, "Leave her alone. She has done a beautiful thing. She has prepared My body for burial."

You will need:

✂

Small glass jar with screw-top lid, such as a spice or herb jar

Paper towels

Ping-Pong® ball

Craft glue and brush

Paints and brush

Metallic craft paints

Small beads, needle and thread for decoration

Remove the lid from the clean glass jar and brush the top with craft glue. Tear up small pieces of paper towel and stick them to the surface. Avoid gluing the paper to the screw top rim.

2 Cover the entire surface of the jar, making sure the paper remains crinkly. Cover the lid, keeping it separate from the jar. Allow to dry. Add more layers to give an extra crinkly texture to the surface.

4 When the jar and lid are completely dry, paint them both. The perfume jar that Mary used was made of alabaster and would have looked very plain, but you can decorate your perfume jar to make it very special. Allow to dry.

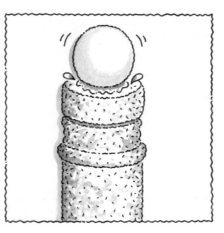

3 Glue the Ping-Pong® ball to the top of the lid and cover it with the glued paper towel so it has a crinkly texture to match the jar.

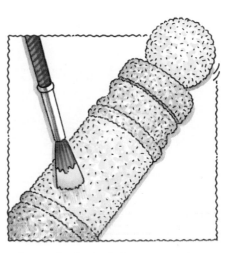

5 To make the jar look very expensive, paint a thin coat of gold or silver paint sparingly over the surface, making sure the first color still shows through.

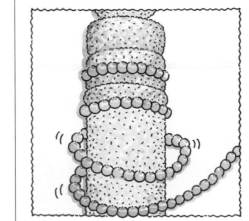

6 Finally, decorate the perfume jar. Thread very small beads onto a length of thread and tie knots in the ends. Wind the thread of beads around the jar and glue them firmly in place.

Make this jar to remind you of Mary's gift to Jesus.

JESUS IS BETRAYED

Judas betrays Jesus for thirty silver coins.

Matthew 26:14–16; Mark 14:10–11; Luke 22:3–6

The chief priests wanted to get rid of Jesus. But they didn't know how to capture Him.

Judas Iscariot, who had been one of Jesus' closest friends, did not love Jesus or want to serve Him. Instead, he did something evil.

Judas went to the chief priests and asked, "What will you pay me if I hand Jesus over to you?"

"We'll give you thirty pieces of silver," they said.

After that, Judas watched for a chance to hand Jesus over to them. Jesus knew what Judas had done, but it did not change His love for all people. Jesus would still suffer and die for the sins of all.

You will need:

✄

TO MAKE THE COINS:

Self-hardening clay

Rolling pin and wooden or plastic board

Toothpicks

Carving tools

Round plastic bottle top

Sheets of paper towels

Silver craft paint and brush

TO MAKE THE MONEY BAG:

6" x 12" piece of felt

Needle, thread, and scissors

16" length of cord

Scraps of felt and beads

1 Using the rolling pin, roll out the clay on the board to an even thickness of about ¼".

2 Use the round plastic lid as a cutter to cut 30 circles from the clay. Carefully remove these clay circles from the board and place them on the paper towel.

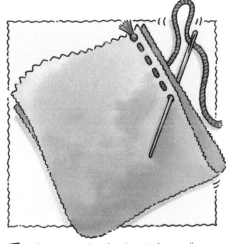

Make these silver coins as a reminder of how Judas turned against Jesus.

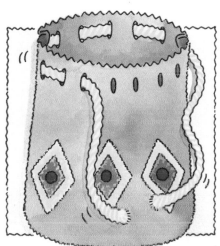

5 Coins were often kept safe in small money bags made from leather or cloth. To make the bag, fold the piece of felt in half and sew along each side using a short, simple, running stitch.

6 Turn the bag inside out so the stitching is on the inside. Glue on scraps of felt and beads to decorate the bag. Ask an adult to use the scissors to make a row of small holes about ¾" from the top. Thread the cord in and out of the holes. Thread a small bead on to each end and tie a knot. Fray the ends, then tie the ends together. Keep your silver coins in the money bag and pull the cord tight to keep them safe.

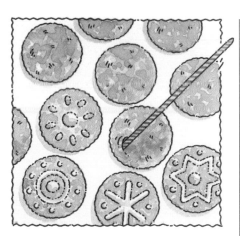

3 Use the toothpicks or tools to decorate the clay circles, making them look like coins. Roman coins were often decorated with the head of the emperor, but you can make your own designs. Try to keep the coins flat and allow them to dry out completely—about one day.

4 When the coins are dry, paint them silver. Paint one side and let dry before turning over to paint the reverse side.

JESUS WASHES HIS DISCIPLES' FEET

Jesus shows His disciples how much He loves them.

John 13:1–17

Jesus knew He would soon die and would not be with His friends much longer. He wanted to celebrate the Passover meal with them one last time. Passover was a special time of remembering how God had rescued Moses and the Israelites from slavery in Egypt many years ago.

Jesus met His 12 friends at the upper room of a house.

He took a bowl of water and began to wash His disciples' feet.

"You mustn't wash my feet!" said Peter. "You are our Master, not our servant!"

"Unless I wash you, you don't belong to Me," said Jesus.

"Then wash my hands and head as well!" said Peter.

Jesus washed Peter's feet.

"Now that I have washed your feet," said Jesus, "you must also wash one another's feet. Do loving tasks for one another as I have done for you." Jesus' life of service continued to the cross where He died for the sins of all people.

You will need:

✂

Large plastic bowl
Newspaper
Craft glue and brush
Plastic wrap and cooking oil
Light brown paint and brush
Scissors
Pictures cut from magazines
Pencil
Spray shellac (optional)

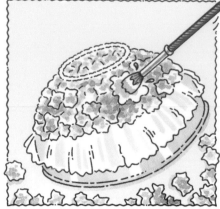

1 Use the plastic bowl as your mold. Lightly grease the outside with the oil and cover with the plastic wrap. Cover the outside of the bowl with six layers of small newspaper pieces glued with diluted glue. The design of this papier-mâché bowl is shallow, so you will only need to cover about 8" up the sides.

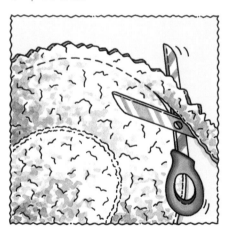

2 Allow the papier-mâché to dry overnight, then remove it from the plastic bowl by pulling away the plastic wrap. Neaten the bowl by trimming around the edges with the scissors.

3 Neaten the edge of the bowl further by gluing small strips of newspaper around the rim. Allow to dry.

4 When it is dry, paint the bowl inside and out with a light brown paint to make the bowl look as if it is made from clay. Decorate the bowl with a simple mosaic pattern. Draw an outline in pencil around the rim of the bowl and include a small design in the center.

5 Cut out lots of small squares from the pictures cut from magazines and arrange all the squares into groups of similar colors to make the mosaics. This design does not cover the bowl completely, but makes a border pattern and center design.

6 Follow the pencil guidelines and glue the paper squares to the surface of the bowl. Build up the mosaic pattern and overlap the squares if necessary. When you have finished decorating the bowl, you can varnish it to help strengthen and protect the mosaic.

Make this mosaic bowl and think about how much Jesus loved His friends.

THE LAST SUPPER

Jesus shares a special meal with His disciples.

Matthew 26:17–30; Mark 14:17–26; Luke 22:14–20

After Jesus had finished washing everyone's feet, He reclined at the table with His disciples, ready to eat the Passover meal.

Jesus said, "One of you is going to hand Me over to be killed."

"Surely not I!" each one said to another.

Make this special cup to remember Jesus' words at the Last Supper.

You will need:

✂

2 clean plastic dessert bowls

Plastic spool

Scissors

Dried beans, peas, and lentils

Paper towel

Tape

Craft glue and brush

Toothpick

Silver or brown paint

Paintbrush

But Jesus already knew it would be Judas Iscariot.

Jesus took the cup of wine, thanked God for it, and offered it to them. "Drink from it, all of you. Do this to remember Me," said Jesus. "This is My blood, for many." Jesus' friends drank the wine.

Then He took the bread, gave thanks, broke it, and gave it to His friends. "Take and eat. Do this to remember Me," said Jesus. "This is My body." The disciples ate the bread.

They sang a song together and then went to the Mount of Olives.

It wouldn't be long until Jesus' body and blood would be sacrificed on the cross for the sins of all people. Today, Jesus gives us His body and blood in Holy Communion.

1 Use the scissors carefully to cut out the bottom section of one of the dessert bowls to form the base of the cup. Tip this upside-down, as shown below. The spool will form the stem of the cup.

2 Glue the spool between the two sections and allow to dry.

3 Brush the surface with glue and cover the bowls with torn pieces of paper towel. The layers of paper towel will help to hold the two plastic bowls and the spool together. Make sure the paper remains nice and crinkly. Cover the whole surface inside and out with at least two layers of paper and allow to dry.

4 Wind yarn or string around the rim of the cup, fixing the string in place with dabs of glue. Then glue string around the stem and the base of the cup and allow to dry.

5 Make a raised pattern on the surface of the cup with dried beans, peas, and lentils. Place small blobs of glue on the surface using the toothpick to carefully position the beans on the glue.

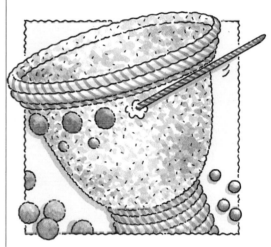

6 When you have finished decorating the cup, allow the glue to dry completely. Then paint the cup inside and out with the silver or brown poster paint. It is likely that the cup Jesus used would have been made of earthenware. Today the cups used for the Lord's Supper in church are usually made of silver.

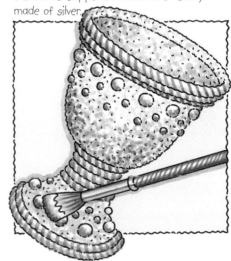

Peter tells lies to save himself.

PETER DENIES JESUS

John 18:15–18, 25–27

Jesus had twelve disciples. One day He warned the disciples that they would leave Him. Peter boasted that he never would, but Jesus knew Peter was going to deny Him three times.

Shortly before Jesus was taken away to be killed, He warned Peter: "Before the cock crows tonight, you will say three times that you do not know Me."

Peter was very upset. Jesus was his friend! But when Jesus was taken away by soldiers, Peter and the other disciples were frightened and ran away.

Later, when Peter was waiting to see what would happen, some people asked if he was a friend of Jesus.

"No," said Peter, "I don't know what you are talking about!"

They asked him three times and each time he said, "No!"

Then a rooster crowed. Peter remembered what Jesus had said.

Peter felt terrible and cried bitterly.

Soon after that Jesus showed His love for Peter and you and me when He died on the cross to take away our sins.

You will need:

✂

Sheet of colored poster board

Glue stick

Sheets of colored paper

Pencil

Scraps of colored wrapping papers

Scissors

1 Sketch out a simple outline of a rooster on the poster board. Draw in the details and features. Draw a border around the edge.

2 Draw lots of different-sized feathers on the colored paper. Follow the shapes on your design and draw the claws and leg and tail feathers. Cut out the shapes carefully.

3 Cut out shapes to make the border and glue them around the edge, following your outline.

4 Use the glue stick to glue the feather shapes onto your sketch. Start with the tail feathers and overlap them, using different colors. Then glue the claw and leg shapes. Cut out shapes for the borders.

5 The body feathers will hide the ends of the tail feathers and the legs. Start at the bottom of the rooster and glue the feathers down. Follow the body shape of the rooster and overlap the feathers as you work up to the neck. Make sure all the background is covered between the feathers.

6 Cut out shapes for the beak and the head feathers and glue in place. Cut a circle for the head and glue that over the top. Then add the eye.

THE FIRST EASTER

Luke 23:33–46; 24:1–12

Jesus dies to save sinners.

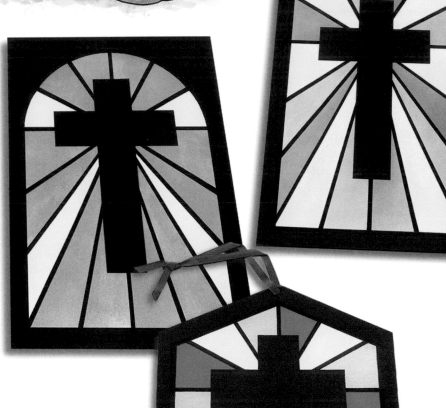

You will need:

Sheets of dark colored cardstock

White paper

Glue stick

Poster paints and brush
or
colored felt-tipped pens

Thick black felt-tipped pen

Scissors

Pencil

Ruler

Make this "stained glass" card for Easter.

Jesus came to earth to save all people from sin. He lived perfectly, but He had many enemies. The enemies arrested Him and had Him put on trial. People accused Jesus and told lies about Him. Finally, the Roman governor, Pilate, told the soldiers to crucify Jesus.

On Good Friday, Jesus was taken by soldiers and nailed to a cross. It was a terrible day. Jesus' mother, Mary, stood close by and watched.

Jesus died. His body was taken down from the cross and placed in a tomb. Jesus' disciples were sad.

But three days later they had an amazing surprise—Jesus came alive again! His friends came to the tomb to see His body, but He had risen! Jesus was alive!

Jesus had won the victory over sin, death, and the devil. Through His victory, Jesus has won eternal life for us.

1 Cut a sheet of white paper in half and trim to make sure the design will fit on the finished card.

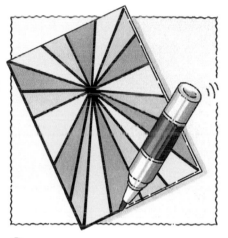

3 Color in the rays with poster paints or felt-tipped pens. Then draw over the original pencil lines with the thick black felt-tipped pen. Also draw a black line around the edge of the design.

5 Use the ruler and pencil to draw a cross shape on the dark cardstock and cut it out. Glue the cross onto the center of the design so the rays shine out from behind the cross.

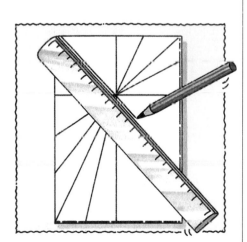

2 Make a central point on the white paper, about 2" from the top. Use the ruler to draw lines radiating out from this point to the edges of the paper.

4 Fold a sheet of cardstock in half. Carefully glue the design to the front of the folded card using the glue stick.

6 Make more cards! Try new shapes, as shown here, with different color schemes. To make a window hanging, you will need only half the sheet of cardstock, but make two cross designs and glue one on each side.

JESUS IS ALIVE!
The empty tomb.
Luke 24:1–12

It was three days since Jesus had died on the cross. All His friends were heartbroken and didn't know what to do next. Some of the women went to his tomb early on Sunday morning, but they had a shock! The large stone which blocked the entrance to the tomb had been rolled away!

Inside the tomb, Jesus' body was gone. All that was left were strips of cloth that the body had been wrapped in. Suddenly two men in bright shining clothes (angels) appeared.

"Don't look for Jesus here," they said. "He's alive! Go quickly and tell His friends."

The women couldn't believe it! They ran home at once and told Jesus' disciples.

Very soon the disciples saw Jesus again for themselves. It was true! Jesus *was* who He said He was—the Son of God. Jesus *did* what He said He would do— die and rise to be a sacrifice for the sins of the world. Jesus was alive!

You will need:

✂

Large, round tin lid or aluminum pizza pan

Black, brown, and white poster paint and brush

Collection of small pieces of dried bark and twigs

Collection of small fresh flowers, leaves, and moss

Collection of different-sized stones and rocks*

Gravel*

Craft glue and brush

Paper towels

* Health and safety precaution: these materials should be washed thoroughly before children handle them.

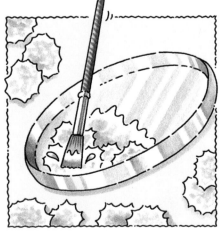

1 First you will need to disguise the shiny tin pan. Tear up small pieces of paper towels and glue them to the inside and rim of the pan with craft glue, giving the surface a rough texture.

2 Make sure the shiny surface is completely covered, especially around the outside of the rim, then allow to dry. Paint the textured surface with brown and white paint, giving it a dappled finish.

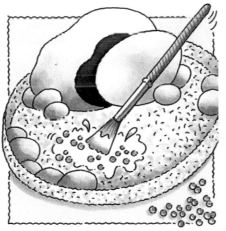

3 The largest rock will represent the tomb. Use the black paint to paint a circular shape on the side of the rock to represent the entrance to the tomb.

4 Position the large rock on the pan and find another rock to represent the stone that would have been rolled in front of the entrance hole. Glue these in place.

5 Arrange the rest of the smaller stones around the edge of the pan and next to the large rocks and glue these in place. Then brush the inside of the pan with glue and sprinkle gravel onto the glue.

Make this Easter garden to show Jesus' victory over death.

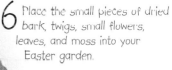

6 Place the small pieces of dried bark, twigs, small flowers, leaves, and moss into your Easter garden.

JESUS PROVIDES BREAKFAST

The risen Jesus appears to His disciples.
John 21:1–14

Over the next few days, Jesus appeared to His disciples, showing them that He really was alive.

One night, Peter and a group of disciples were out fishing in their boat. They had caught nothing. Early the next morning, Jesus stood on the shore, watching them. He was far away, so they couldn't see at first who it was.

"Friends, haven't you caught any fish?" He shouted to the fishermen.

"No!" they said.

"Then throw your net on the other side of the boat," said Jesus. "You will catch fish!"

They did as He said and sure enough, their nets were filled with wriggling fish.

"It's the Lord!" said Peter. They knew that only Jesus could do something so amazing. Peter was so excited that he jumped out of the boat and swam to shore.

Jesus had made a small fire on the shore. He was ready to cook some of the fish. He had some bread for them too. His disciples sat with Him and ate breakfast on the beach.

Just as Jesus provided help and food for His disciples that day, He would continue to provide for all their needs both on earth and in heaven. He provides the same things for us too in His Word and the Sacraments.

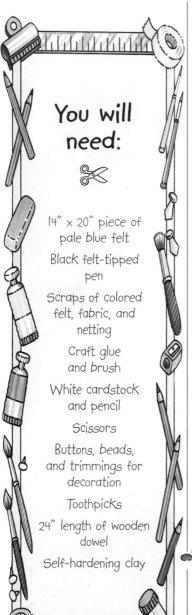

You will need:

14" x 20" piece of pale blue felt

Black felt-tipped pen

Scraps of colored felt, fabric, and netting

Craft glue and brush

White cardstock and pencil

Scissors

Buttons, beads, and trimmings for decoration

Toothpicks

24" length of wooden dowel

Self-hardening clay

Draw one large and one small fish shape on the cardstock. Cut the card shapes out carefully.

Fish are a symbol for Jesus. Make this wall hanging to show that you believe in Jesus.

5 Cut two strips of fabric to fit along the two sides of the hanging and glue these in place. Then glue the small fish on top of these strips to make the border patterns. If you have any small buttons or beads, use them to decorate the fish.

2 Lay the fish patterns on the fabric, draw around them with the felt-tipped pen, and cut them out. You will need two large fish and eight small ones. If you have a selection of fabrics, use different colors and patterns.

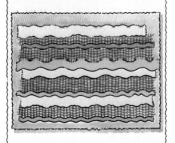

3 Cut several wavy strips of colored fabric and glue them across the background to make an underwater scene. Use blue, gray, and green netting and wavy trimmings. Don't worry about lining up the ends of the wavy strips along the two sides as these will be covered by the border pattern.

4 Glue the two large fish to the center of the scene, on the top of the waves. Cut out several fabric circles and glue them to the bodies of the fish to represent their scales.

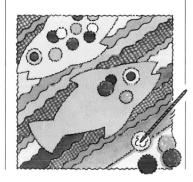

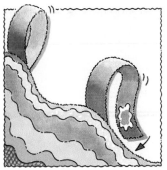

6 Cut four strips of fabric to make loops along the top of the hanging and glue in place. Thread the wooden dowel through the loops. Make two clay balls. Push a clay ball on each end of the dowel to hold the hanging in place. Paint the clay balls after they are dry.

PENTECOST
The Holy Spirit comes in power

Use this book to write prayers thanking God for His gifts. Ask His Spirit to work in the hearts of others.

Acts 2:1–41

You will need:

✂

A small notebook

Ruler

Brightly colored paper

Selection of neon, metallic, or holographic papers in yellows, golds, and fiery colors

Scissors

Glue stick

Small strips of cardstock for the bookmarks

Pentecost, or the Feast of Weeks, was a Jewish festival marking the beginning of harvest. It was at this time that the Holy Spirit came, just as Jesus had said. As the disciples were gathered in Jerusalem, a sound like the rushing of a mighty wind filled the whole house and tongues of fire came to rest on each of them.

The disciples, full of the Holy Spirit, then spoke in many different languages and people from different countries

1 Take the notebook and measure the width and the length of the front cover. Subtract ¼" from both measurements to give you the size of the front panel.

3 Draw different sizes of "tongues of fire" shapes. Use the colored foils and holographic papers if you have them, as they will make the tongues of fire sparkle and glow. Cut out the flames.

5 Finally, cut out the very smallest flames and glue them in place.

2 Cut a piece of brightly colored paper to the size of the front panel measurements. This will be the background. Stick the paper to the front of the notebook using the glue stick.

4 Glue the large flames to the cover first. Build up the design, gluing smaller shapes on top. Use contrasting colors and textures and place different papers on top of each other.

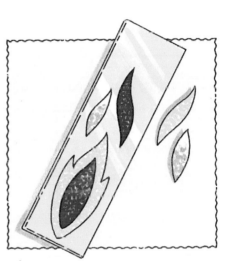

6 Use the small piece of cardstock to make the bookmark. Decorate it with flame shapes to match the notebook.

each understood what was being said about Jesus in their own language. The apostle Peter began to powerfully preach to the crowds about Jesus and how He forgave repentant sinners. Through the power of the Holy Spirit, many people believed and were baptized that very day.

The Holy Spirit calls and gathers people into the church on earth. He works through the Word of God preached and taught and through the Sacraments.

Where to find the stories in the Bible

God made the world
Genesis 1:1-3

Noah's ark
Genesis 6:1-9:17

The tower of Babel
Genesis 11:1-9

God's promise to Abraham
Genesis 15:1-6; 17:1-7

Rebekah's surprise
Genesis 24:10-67

Jacob and Esau
Genesis 25:27-35

Joseph's coat
Genesis 37:3

Joseph's dreams
Genesis 37:1-11

Joseph interprets dreams
Genesis 40:1-23

Moses in the bulrushes
Exodus 2:1-10

The golden lampstand
Exodus 25:31-40

Gideon's victory
Judges 6:1-7:25

The strength of Samson
Judges 14:5-6; 16:4-30

David's harp
1 Samuel 16:14-23

David and Goliath
1 Samuel 17:4-50

Daniel in the lions' den
Daniel 6

Jonah and the big fish
Jonah 1-2

An angel visits Mary
Luke 1:26-38

Mary and Joseph
travel to Bethlehem
Luke 2:1-5

Bethlehem is full
Luke 2:1-7

Jesus is born
Luke 2:6-7

The shepherds' surprise
Luke 2:8-20

Shepherds go to find Jesus
Luke 2:16-20

Jesus is presented in the temple
Luke 2:21-32

A new star in the sky
Matthew 2:1-2

Gifts for the baby King
Matthew 2:9-12

The Christmas story
Matthew 2:1-12; Luke 1:26-2:20

Jesus is baptized
Matthew 3:13-17

The temptation of Jesus
Matthew 4:1-11; Mark 1:12-13; Luke 4:1-13

The wedding at Cana
John 2:1-11

The centurion's faith
Luke 7:1-10

The storm on the lake
Matthew 8:23-27

Loaves and fishes
John 6:1-15

The good seed
Luke 8:5-15

Hidden treasure
Matthew 13:44

The wise and foolish girls
Matthew 25:1-13

The lost coin
Luke 15:8-10

Jesus enters Jerusalem
Matthew 21:1-11

Jesus clears the temple
Matthew 21:12-13; Mark 11:15-18;
Luke 19:45-47

Jesus is anointed
Matthew 26:6-13; Mark 14:3-9

Jesus is betrayed
Matthew 26:14-16; Mark 14:10-11;
Luke 22:3-6

Jesus washes His disciples' feet
John 13:1-17

The Last Supper
Matthew 26:17-30; Mark 14:17-26;
Luke 22:14-20

Peter denies Jesus
John 18:15-18, 25-27

The first Easter
Luke 23:33-46; 24:1-12

Jesus is alive!
Luke 24:1-12

Jesus provides breakfast
John 21:1-14

Pentecost
Acts 2:1-41

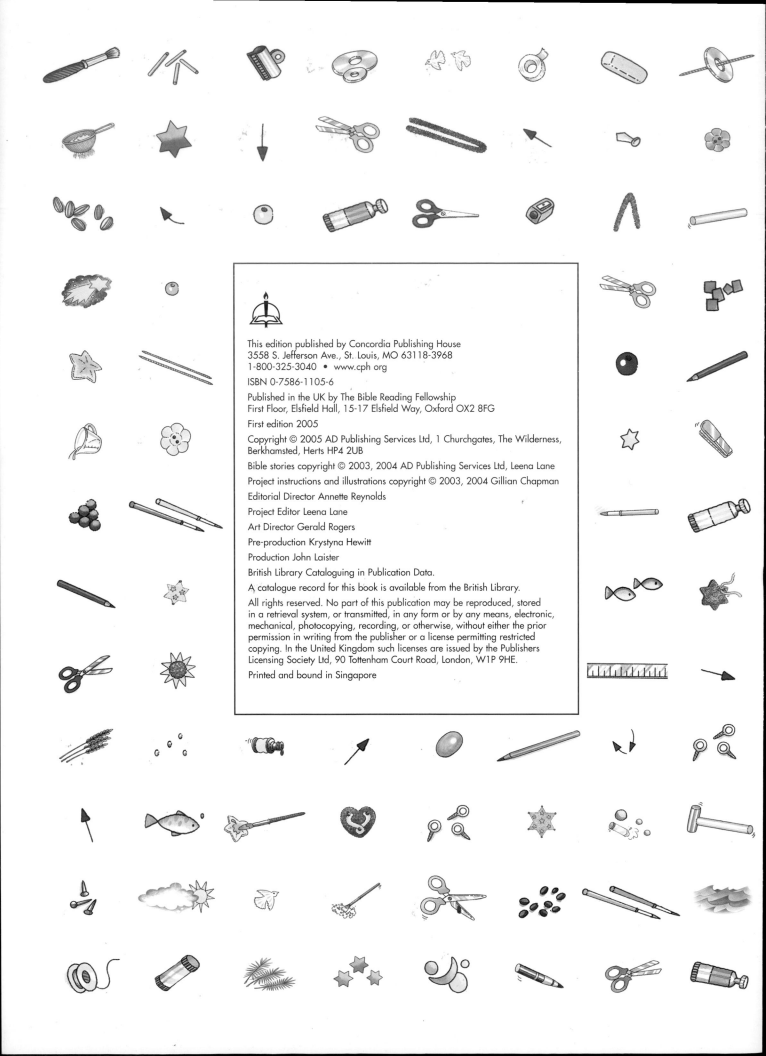

This edition published by Concordia Publishing House
3558 S. Jefferson Ave., St. Louis, MO 63118-3968
1-800-325-3040 • www.cph.org

ISBN 0-7586-1105-6

Published in the UK by The Bible Reading Fellowship
First Floor, Elsfield Hall, 15-17 Elsfield Way, Oxford OX2 8FG

First edition 2005

Copyright © 2005 AD Publishing Services Ltd, 1 Churchgates, The Wilderness,
Berkhamsted, Herts HP4 2UB

Bible stories copyright © 2003, 2004 AD Publishing Services Ltd, Leena Lane

Project instructions and illustrations copyright © 2003, 2004 Gillian Chapman

Editorial Director Annette Reynolds

Project Editor Leena Lane

Art Director Gerald Rogers

Pre-production Krystyna Hewitt

Production John Laister

British Library Cataloguing in Publication Data.

A catalogue record for this book is available from the British Library.

Printed and bound in Singapore